A. J. Wentworth, B.A.

"A splendid comic hero . . . this wonderfully earnest, humourless, and largely ineffective man, for all his pomposity and constant concern with trivialities cannot fail to engage the sympathy of everyone who has ever sat in a classroom either as master or pupil . . . Few books have made me laugh out loud quite so often, yet for all that A. J. is a man after my own heart"
Christopher Matthew, *Evening Standard*

"A prospective reader need only be warned that this is not a book he will read without bursting into frequent fits of laughter – very embarrassing if you are in a crowd. There can be no higher recommendation. I advise you to suffer this fool at the earliest opportunity . . . very gladly"
Manchester Evening News

"Masterly caricature . . . One laughs so often and so loud at the pompous twitchings and fussing of Mr Ellis's retired bachelor preparatory schoolmaster that one feels almost guilty"
Times Educational Supplement

"Wentworth turns out to be the hero of a work certain to be pigeon-holed as a minor classic by which people usually mean a classic more readable than the major kind . . . a man Mr Pooter would regard with awe but nevertheless recognise as a brother"
Benny Green, *The Spectator*

"A great English eccentric"
Sunday Telegraph

. F. Ellis

. J. Wentworth, B.A.

ntaining THE PAPERS OF A. J. WENTWORTH, B.A.
d THE PAPERS OF A. J. WENTWORTH, B.A. (RET'D)

rrow Books

Arrow Books Limited
17–21 Conway Street, London WIP 5HL

An imprint of the Hutchinson Publishing Group

London Melbourne Sydney Auckland
Johannesburg and agencies
throughout the world

First published by Weidenfeld and Nicolson 1980
Arrow edition 1981
Reprinted 1981 (twice)
© H. F. Ellis, 1949, 1962, 1980

The material in this book is adapted from articles which
originally appeared in *Punch*

Subsequently published in two separate books as
THE PAPERS OF A. J. WENTWORTH, B.A.
by Evans Brothers, 1949, and
A. J. WENTWORTH, B.A. (RET'D)
by Geoffrey Bles, 1962

Published in Penguin Books 1964

Made and printed in Great Britain
by The Anchor Press Ltd
Tiptree, Essex

ISBN 0 09 925990 7

Contents

Introduction

tempts to persuade my old friend Arthur James Wentworth
allow me to give to the public certain hitherto unrecorded
sodes in his not unremarkable career – a visit to the United
ates, for instance, and the story of his acquittal on a charge of
ving a motor-mower without due care and attention – have
far proved unsuccessful. 'Plenty of time, plenty of time,' he is
t to say; 'these decisions must not be rushed.' Now in his
hty-third year (assuming, that is, that we are to take as
rrect an impertinent observation made by the boy Atkins as
ng ago as July 1939), though he looks younger, Mr Went-
orth seems oblivious of the passage of the years. It is not for me
remind him that the Great Reaper, unlike the boys of Set
IA at Burgrove cannot be kept indefinitely at bay by a dis-
ssive glance.

He has, however, consented to the republication of his papers
(in his own phrase) 'occasional jottings', which first saw the
ht in book form at intervals between 1949 and 1962. A whole
w generation of schoolmasters has grasped the chalk since
ose distant days and, from all Mr Wentworth hears and reads,
adly in need of such guidance as an experienced old hand can
ve. In particular, the monstrous misconception that in no
cumstances is a master justified in throwing books etc. at his
ys – the heresy that originally decided him to give the benefit
his own experience to the profession – has if anything grown
ore widespread since his retirement. On occasion, after read-
g of some teacher reprimanded or even dismissed by what he
lls a 'set of ignorant busybodies' for nothing more than a
aightforward disciplinary swipe, Mr Wentworth expresses
mself with unaccustomed violence. 'God bless my soul!' he
s been heard to say.

The original publication of the first part of the present b⸢ook⸣
for which I endeavoured to select, at his request, only s⸢uch⸣
material as threw light on the forces militating against the c⸢om⸣
posure and, indeed, the sanity of assistant masters, led to s⸢ome⸣
misguided criticism of his character and general outlook on ⸢life.⸣
In particular he resented the suggestion, made by several ⸢cor⸣
respondents, that he was 'just a typical narrow-minded sch⸢ool⸣
master', with no ideas or interests beyond time-tables, squ⸢are⸣
brackets and Matron's concern for the boys' socks. Eventua⸢lly,⸣
after his retirement, he felt it his duty, if only in fairness to ⸢his⸣
profession, to counter these damaging misconceptions, ⸢and⸣
accordingly sent me a further instalment of personal jotti⸢ngs,⸣
cuttings from local papers, theatre-ticket stubs, travel literat⸢ure⸣
and, for some reason, a bulb catalogue with 'Narrow-min⸢ded⸣
my foot!' scrawled across the cover. 'Do what you like w⸢ith⸣
these,' he wrote, 'as long as you give a fair picture of my life ⸢and⸣
philosophy of living, both here at Fenport and on my, I thi⸢nk I⸣
may claim, fairly extensive travels. I make no explicit defenc⸢e or⸣
apologia. It appears to me that a simple, straightforw⸢ard⸣
account of my life, as I live it in retirement from day to d⸢ay,⸣
should suffice to show that, for variety and breadth of intere⸢st,⸣
civic sense, tolerance and a readiness to meet and mingle w⸢ith⸣
all sorts and conditions of men and (up to a point of cou⸢rse)⸣
women, a retired schoolmaster can hold a candle to any T⸢om,⸣
Dick or Harry.'

Here then, with the addition of a couple of notes kindly s⸢ent⸣
me by his colleague Mr Gilbert which clear up one or t⸢wo⸣
points left in some obscurity by my old friend, is the first-ha⸢nd⸣
record of A. J. Wentworth at work and play (and, indeed, ⸢at⸣
war) – a record upon which he is content, he tells me, to let ⸢his⸣
reputation stand or fall before the bar of public opinion. ⸢He⸣
himself, I ought to add, remains in no doubt whatever of ⸢the⸣
verdict.

H. F. ELLIS

Kingston St Mary, Somerset 1979

The Papers of
A. J. Wentworth, B.A.

Statement of
Arthur James Wentworth, B.A.

My name is Arthur James Wentworth, I am unmarried and I am by profession an assistant master at Burgrove Preparatory School, Wilminster. The Headmaster is the Reverend Gregory Saunders, M.A. He is known to the boys as the Squid – not necessarily, I think, a term of opprobrium. He is a classical scholar of moderate attainments, a generous employer and much given to the use of the expression, 'The School must come first, Wentworth.' I attach no particular meaning to this remark.

At 11.15 on the morning of Saturday 8 July, I entered Classroom 4 for the purpose of instructing Set IIIA in Algebra. There were present Anderson, Atkins, Clarke, Etheridge, Hillman, Hopgood II, Mason, Otterway, Sapoulos, Trench and Williamson. Heathcote, who has, I am told, a boil, was absent. It should be explained that though I have given these names in the alphabetical order in which they appear in the school list, that is not the order in which the boys were sitting on this occasion. It is the custom at Burgrove for boys to sit according to their position in the previous week's mark-lists. Thus in the front row were seated Etheridge, a most promising mathematician, Hillman, Mason, Otterway and Clarke. Hopgood II, the boy whom I am now accused of assaulting, was in the middle of the second row. The third and last row was shared by Sapoulos, a Greek, and Atkins, a cretin. I do not think these facts have any bearing on anything that is to follow, but I give them for the sake of completeness.

'This morning,' I remarked, taking up my *Hall and Knight*, 'we will do problems,' and I told them at once that if there was any more of that groaning they would do nothing but problems for the next month. It is my experience, as an assistant master of some years' standing, that if groaning is not checked immediately it may swell to enormous proportions. I make it my business to stamp on it.

Mason, a fair-haired boy with glasses, remarked when the groaning had died down that it would not be possible to do problems for the next month, and on being asked why not replied that there were only three weeks more of term. This was true, and I decided to make no reply. He then asked if he could have a mark for that. I said, 'No, Mason, you may not,' and, taking up my book and a piece of chalk, read out, 'I am just half as old as my father and in twenty years I shall be five years older than he was twenty years ago. How old am I?' Atkins promptly replied, 'Forty-two.' I inquired of him how, unless he was gifted with supernatural powers, he imagined he could produce the answer without troubling to do any working-out. He said, 'I saw it in the *Schools Year-book*.' This stupid reply caused a great deal of laughter, which I suppressed.

I should have spoken sharply to Atkins, but at this moment I noticed that his neighbour Sapoulos, the Greek boy, appeared to be eating toffee, a practice which is forbidden at Burgrove during school hours. I ordered him to stand up. 'Sapoulos,' I said, 'you are not perhaps quite used yet to our English ways, and I shall not punish you this time for your disobedience; but please understand that I will not have eating in my class. You did not come here to eat but to learn. If you try hard and pay attention, I do not altogether despair of teaching you something, but if you do not wish to learn I cannot help you. You might as well go back to your own country.' Mason, without being given permission to speak, cried excitedly, 'He can't, sir. Didn't you know? His father was chased out of Greece in a revolution or something. A big man with a black beard chased him for three miles and he had to escape in a small boat. It's true, sir. You ask him. Sapoulos got hit on the knee with a brick, didn't you, Sappy? And his grandmother – at least I think it was his grandmother –'

'That will do, Mason,' I said. 'Who threw that?'

I am not, I hope, a martinet, but I will not tolerate the

throwing of paper darts, or other missiles in my algebra set. Some of the boys make small pellets out of their blotting-paper and flick them with their garters. This sort of thing has to be put down with a firm hand or work becomes impossible. I accordingly warned the boy responsible that another offence would mean an imposition. He had the impertinence to ask what sort of an imposition. I said that it would be a pretty stiff imposition, and if he wished to know more exact details he had only to throw another dart to find out. He thereupon threw another dart.

I confess that at this I lost patience and threatened to keep the whole set in during the afternoon if I had any more trouble. The lesson then proceeded.

It was not until I had completed my working out of the problem on the board that I realized I had worked on the assumption – of course ridiculous – that I was *twice* my father's age instead of *half*. This gave the false figure of minus 90 for my own age. Some boy said, 'Crikey!' I at once whipped round and demanded to know who had spoken. Otterway suggested that it might have been Hopgood II talking in his sleep. I was about to reprimand Otterway for impertinence when I realized that Hopgood actually was asleep and had in fact, according to Williamson, been asleep since the beginning of the period. Mason said, 'He hasn't missed much, anyway.'

I then threw my *Hall and Knight*. It has been suggested that it was intended to hit Hopgood II. This is false. I never wake up sleeping boys by throwing books at them, as hundreds of old Burgrove boys will be able to testify. I intended to hit Mason, and it was by a mischance which I shall always regret that Hopgood was struck. I have had, as I told my Headmaster, a great deal to put up with from Mason, and no one who knows the boy blames me for the attempt to do him some physical violence. It is indeed an accepted maxim in the Common Room that physical violence is the only method of dealing with Mason which produces any results; to this the Headmaster some time ago added a rider that the boy be instructed to remove his spectacles before being assaulted. That I forgot to do this must be put down to the natural agitation of a mathematics master caught out in an error. But I blame myself for it.

I do not blame myself for the unfortunate stunning of Hopgood II. It was an accident. I did all I could for the boy when it was discovered (I think by Etheridge) that he had been rendered unconscious. I immediately summoned the Headmaster and we talked the matter over. We agreed that concealment was impossible that that I must give a full account of the circumstances to the police. Meanwhile the work of the school was to go on as usual; Hopgood himself would have wished it. The Headmaster added that in any case the School must come first.

I have made this statement after being duly cautioned, of my own free will and in the presence of witnesses. I have read it through three times with considerable satisfaction, and am prepared to state on oath that it is a true and full account of the circumstances leading up to the accident to Hopgood II. I wish only to add that the boy is now none the worse for the blow, and has indeed shown increased zeal for his studies since the occurrence.

(*Signed*) A. J. WENTWORTH, B.A.

July 1939

Christmas Term 1938
A Routine Week

This has been an unsatisfactory day. When I entered Classroom 4 after break I found the whole class clustered round my desk and immediately ordered them sharply to go to their places and open their books. 'Didn't you hear the bell?' I cried. 'It went two minutes ago.' Some of the boys turned round as I spoke, and I saw to my surprise that they were not IIIA, as I had expected, but the Upper Fourth, and that the Headmaster was seated at the desk correcting their exercises. I am not at all convinced that it is a wise practice to call all the boys up when one is correcting. I have tried it myself with IIIA and also with the Lower Third for English History and it does not work. The boys are inclined to jostle for places, and on one occasion IIIA pushed my desk, through over-keenness, right off its dais, with the result that a great deal of ink was spilled and Etheridge, the best worker of the lot, sprained his wrist and had to go up to Matron. But of course a headmaster has the right to do as he likes.

As soon as I realized my mistake I apologized.

'I beg your pardon, Headmaster,' I said, colouring, 'I was thinking it was Monday.'

'It *is* Monday, Mr Wentworth,' he said kindly.

There was no more to be said, so I apologized again and withdrew. I should have remembered that on Mondays I take IIIA in Room 6, since the Library, where the Headmaster ordinarily takes the Upper Fourth, is wanted by Miss Coombes for her Music now that the Music Room is used for P.T. on wet days.

On my way down the corridor to Room 6 I remembered

that I had forgotten to bring IIIA's corrected books with me and hurried back to the Common Room to get them. There I found Gilbert smoking a pipe. 'Hullo, A.J.,' he said. 'I thought you were having fun with IIIA this period.' I explained that I was looking for some exercise-books and asked if he had seen them.

'There were some old books on the table this morning,' he said; 'but I burnt those. I thought they were finished with.'

I was nearly taken in for a moment, but I know C.G. of old. 'You're pulling my leg, C.G.,' I said, doubling up my fists in pretended anger; and sure enough soon found my books at the back of my locker.

This incident delayed me still further, and in my haste to get to work I inadvertently returned to Room 4 instead of Room 6. Not wishing, naturally, to disturb the Headmaster a second time, I closed the door again as quietly as I could the moment I heard his voice conjugating the imperfect subjunctive passive of 'audio', but even so could not help hearing him say, 'See who that was, Briggs.' I now made what proved to be the fatal mistake of running into the boot-room. This little room, in which, as the name implies, the boys keep their boots and shoes, lies on the right of a narrow passage running off the main corridor almost opposite Classroom 4, and it was natural that it should come into my mind, since the main corridor itself continues for a considerable distance on either side of Room 4 without offering concealment of any kind.

Time and again I have warned the school boot-boy not to leave the large basket, in which he collects the soiled shoes for cleaning, in the middle of the boot-room floor. It is an unnecessary obstruction, and what is more I have known boys turn it upside-down and hide under it when I have been marshalling them for a Sunday afternoon walk. But the boot-boy has, I am afraid, about as much sense as Atkins, who is easily the stupidest of my IIIA boys. I fell over, and indeed into, this basket with a considerable noise, and in so doing lost hold of my exercise-books, which flew all over the room. I was still in this ludicrous position, striving to free my gown which had caught in the wickerwork, when Briggs put his head round the door, said 'Golly!' and disappeared again, no doubt to report what he had seen to the Headmaster.

It can be imagined that I was in no mood after this to stand any nonsense from anybody, and IIIA found that they had a very different person to deal with this morning from their usual good-natured master. I kept Anderson standing up for twenty minutes and gave Mason the shock of his life by setting him fifty lines for singing. A little severity now and then does them no harm at all.

The Headmaster sent for me after lunch and was very decent about it, though obviously displeased.

'I understand, Wentworth,' he said, 'that you were seen sitting in a basket in the boot-room this morning at a time when you should have been supervising the work of one of your mathematical sets?'

I nodded my head and said eagerly that I could explain.

He said, 'No explanation is necessary. I do not make it my business, as you know, to pry into the affairs of my masters. I trust you all implicitly. But I must make it clear that I cannot allow any master to fritter away, in the boot-room or anywhere else, time which should be devoted to the instruction of my boys. That is what we are all here for – to teach.'

I told him that I was extremely sorry for what had occurred, and added that I was prepared, if he wished it, to give an undertaking never to enter the boot-room again. He replied that he did not wish it, that he hoped I had enough self-control to make such an undertaking unnecessary, and that he had no objection whatever to my going into the boot-room whenever I wished provided that neither the work of the boys nor the dignity of my position was endangered by my presence there. He then said that the School must come first, and I realized that the interview was at an end.

On my way back to the Common Room I met Mason and let him off his imposition. It had worried me to think that I might perhaps have let a momentary irritation override my sense of fair play.

TUESDAY

Every mathematics master dreads the day when he will have to explain the Theorem of Pythagoras to boys who have never met it before. Term after term I get this same feeling of helplessness. The whole thing is ridiculous. With co-operation and proper attention even a dull form should be able to grasp the principles involved and the main lines of the proof in an hour's good hard work; knowledge of the construction will come with practice. But IIIA do *not* co-operate. They are too prone to let their minds wander, to be led astray by what are from the point of view of geometry only side-issues, to *make*, as I am always telling them, difficulties instead of going straight at the task and getting it done. It is not that they are lazy. That I could deal with, for I come down like a ton of bricks on idleness in any shape or form. It is rather, I think, a failure to understand the *importance* of what it is we are trying to do.

'This morning,' I said to them, 'we are going to prove that the square on the hypotenuse of a right-angled triangle is equal to the sum of the squares on the other two sides.'

'Is that a likely thing to happen?' Mason asked.

I told the others to be quiet and asked Mason what he meant.

'I mean is a right-angled triangle likely to have a square on its hypotenuse?'

'I'm afraid I don't quite follow you, Mason,' I said. 'If I draw a right-angled triangle on the board and then draw a square on the side opposite the right angle, it has got a square on its hypotenuse. The question whether it is *likely* to have such a square does not arise.'

'Not on the board, sir, no. But I mean in real life. I mean if real-life triangles don't have squares on their hypotenuses there wouldn't be much point in proving that they are equal to whatever it is they are equal to, would it, sir?'

'You mean "would *there*", you chump.'

'Be quiet, Etheridge,' I said.

'I see what Mason means, sir,' said Hillman. 'I mean it

would be a pretty good fluke if a triangle had squares on all its three sides at once, wouldn't it, sir?'

'There is no question of a fluke about it,' I said, beginning to lose patience. 'Now attend to me, all of you.' I then drew on the board a right-angled triangle ABC, and on the sides AB, AC and BC proceeded to construct squares ABDE, ACFG and BCHJ respectively.

'What is there funny about that, Atkins?' I asked when I had finished.

'Nothing,' he said.

'Then why laugh?'

It is a constant vexation to me that these boys seem to be amused at nothing at all. I do not want them to be glum and dispirited, of course; there are times when we all have a good laugh together and no harm is done. But this inane giggling at nothing simply holds up the work of the set. I gave Atkins a sharp warning and turned to Mason.

'Now, Mason,' I said, 'that wasn't very difficult, was it? My triangle's got squares on each of its sides.'

'My canary's got circles under its eyes,' sang a voice, and there was an immediate outburst of laughter at this piece of downright impertinence.

'Was that you, Williamson?' I demanded sternly.

'No, sir.'

'Then who was it?'

There was no reply.

'Filthy Dick passed the window just then, sir,' suggested Clarke, who sits by it. 'It must have been him.'

'He,' said Etheridge.

'You shut up, Etheridge. You don't know everything.'

'Clarke,' I cried, 'you will come and see me at the end of the period. And you too, Etheridge. I will not have these interruptions.'

'He meant the gardener's boy,' explained Mason. 'We call him Filthy Dick because he never washes. You should see his neck.'

'Never mind that now, Mason. The point is, are you pre-

pared to admit that this figure on the board is a triangle wit
squares on each of its sides?'

'I suppose so, sir. Only it looks more like three squares joine
together now, with a space in the middle.'

'Very well, Mason,' I said wearily. 'Let us put it that whe
three squares have their corners touching in such a way tha
the space enclosed between them is a right-angled triangle, th
largest square is equal to the sum of the two smaller square:
Will that satisfy you?'

'All right by me, sir,' said Mason.

'Anything to get rid of the hypotenuse,' said Anderson.

I threw my chalk into a corner and went quietly to my desk

'You will all,' I said, 'open your books and copy out th
construction and proof of the Theorem of Pythagoras. An
boy who has not finished when the bell rings will complete th
work in his spare time and show it up to me during break
tomorrow morning. I am thoroughly dissatisfied with th
behaviour of the whole set. Unless there is a decided improve
ment in the next few days you will find yourselves in pretty
serious trouble. Now get on with your work in silence. Well
Atkins, what is it?'

'I think Sapoulos is crying again, sir.'

The Greek boy Sapoulos is a source of continual worry to
me. The slightest thing seems to upset him. Naturally one
makes allowances, as he is a stranger in a strange land and may
often feel rather lonely, but it is quite ridiculous that he should
break down over the most trivial matters in the way he does. I
have tried being kind to him but it only seems to make matters
worse, and I dare say what he really needs is a little sternness
and discipline. Something to stiffen him up. On this occasion
I told him not to be so silly, and asked him what the Spartans
at Thermopylae would have thought of such a cry-baby.

I had forgotten, until Mason asked me what the Spartans
did at Thermopylae, that none of my IIIA boys knows any
Greek history. I told him how Leonidas and his gallant three
hundred held a mighty Persian host at bay for days and finally
died at their post rather than surrender.

'What were the Persians up to?' asked Etheridge.

I told him of Xerxes' plans to conquer Greece, and, as the boys were obviously interested, went on to describe the marshalling of the great army, the digging of the canal at Athos, the lashing of the Hellespont with chains and the building of the bridge of boats, and how Xerxes wept to think that of all his host not one man would be alive when a hundred years had passed by. I had got Xerxes as far as Therma, where the river Echeidorus was drunk dry, when to my great disappointment the bell rang. I think the boys were disappointed too, for they asked me quite eagerly to go on with the story another time.

Tomorrow we must have a real go at Pythagoras. I might begin perhaps by telling them something of the man himself and his position in the hierarchy of Greek philosophers.

WEDNESDAY

This morning IIIA were unusually quiet when I went in and I at once glanced at the front legs of my desk. Once or twice since I first came to Burgrove I have hurt myself rather badly through my desk falling off its dais the moment I have leant my elbows on it. I shall always believe, though I have never been able to prove it, that this must have been the work of the boys. Old Poole, who left us last year after twenty-seven years' faithful service in charge of French and Geography, had the same experience, and he was positive that the front legs had been balanced deliberately on the very edge of the dais. Though, as he used to say, it might simply be carelessness on the part of the cleaner. It is always difficult to bring this kind of thing home to the boys.

However, the desk looked all right today, but I was still uneasy. Every schoolmaster knows how unnerving it is when the boys sit quietly in their places and watch you in that silly expressionless way they have, and I do not mind admitting that I stood quite still in the middle of the floor for a full minute waiting for something to happen. Nothing happened at all except that I distinctly heard Mason whispering, '*Rigor mortis* has set in.'

I at once strode to the desk to get my punishment-book, but when I opened the lid a pigeon flew out, nearly knocking my spectacles off and giving me, naturally enough, a very nasty shock. In my seven years at Burgrove I have never had such a thing happen to me. I went white with anger.

'Stop that noise this instant!' I shouted. 'And you, Mason, leave that bird alone and go back to your desk. Now, which of you is responsible for this? Hurry up, I'm waiting.'

There was absolute silence for some seconds, until the pigeon, which had settled on top of the blackboard, began to coo in an annoying way, and I then brought my fist down with a crash on the desk.

'We had better understand one another,' I said with cold fury. 'Somebody put that pigeon in my desk and I am going to find out who did it. Unless the person responsible owns up within three minutes – Ah, Mason, so it *was* you?'

'*Me,* sir. No, sir. Only I think – '

'Well?'

'I think it's got something tied to its leg.'

Someone suggested it might be a message.

'It's a stool-pigeon!' cried Clarke.

'I bet it's spies.'

'Atkins saw a man just like Hitler behind the pavvy – '

'Be quiet!' I shouted.

While I was considering what to do, Mason, who seems utterly unable to hold his tongue for two seconds, asked whether he might find out what the message said. I asked him rather sarcastically how he proposed to catch the pigeon, and before I could object he went to the blackboard and held out his right index finger, which the bird at once settled upon. I gave Hillman fifty lines for clapping, as a warning to the others, and then suggested to Mason that he seemed to know the pigeon remarkably well. He replied that he knew all the school pigeons well and he thought this must be one of them. I had already guessed this, but said nothing.

'Shall I read the message, sir?' he asked, untying it from the bird's leg.

'Very well,' I said, after a moment's hesitation. 'What does it say?'

'It says "Fly at once. All is discovered." '

In the ordinary way I might have joined in the general ghter, but this morning I felt too upset and angry.

'Give me that paper, Mason,' I said, 'and sit down. No – that bird out of the window first. I want every boy – give : some slips, Etheridge, please, there is no need to waste a ole sheet – I want every boy to copy out what is written e and sign his name beneath it. And no talking.'

'Need *I* do it, sir?'

'Certainly you must do it, Sapoulos. And stop that silly impering this instant.'

The boys then began clamouring that they had forgotten message, and to save further trouble I wrote it up on the ard. My plan was of course to compare the handwriting on slips of paper with that on the original paper; in this way elt certain of being able to spot the culprit, though as a atter of fact, when I looked through the slips this evening I and that the boys had misunderstood my intention and itten the words in capitals, which made the test practically eless. Etheridge collected the slips without incident and I en told the whole set to get on with the solving of brackets Exercise 37. I felt too weary and disheartened to do any tual teaching.

Unless someone has owned up by tomorrow morning I shall ve to take severe measures. But it is difficult to know what do.

IURSDAY

here was an unfortunate sequel to the pigeon affair this orning. After prayers in Big School the Headmaster said he d something serious to say. It appears that when he entered lassroom 4 for the second period yesterday morning he found hat he described as an impertinent message scrawled up on e board. He did not propose to repeat the message, as the oy responsible would know very well what he meant. Let that oy stand up at once and confess. I had no option but to come rward from my place with the other masters and explain that had myself written the sentence and that I regretted the ard had not been cleaned at the end of the period by the

bottom boy of the set, whose duty it was. I added, for I did
wish to get Sapoulos into trouble, that the boy concerned
not yet perhaps had time to get used to our English ways
customs.

This ended the matter for the time being, but it has put
in something of a dilemma. The Headmaster, who is, if a
thing, a shade too inquisitive, will no doubt require a fu
explanation, and though I have managed to avoid him for
whole of today, I cannot hope to do so indefinitely. The d
culty is that I do not wish to tell him about the pigeon in
desk; it would only worry him and could do no good. H
still rather upset, to tell the truth, about my accident in
boot-room. So I shall have to think of some other reason
writing that absurd message on the board. It would be be
of course if I could link it up in some way with algebra. B
don't at the moment see my way.

In the meantime I have told IIIA that I have decided to
no more about the pigeon provided nothing of the sort happ
again, and I have warned them that the less they say abou
to anyone the better it will be for them.

It looks as if I may have to go to the Headmaster over this
with Gilbert about his wretched potatoes. Important as
crop may be, there are other things in the world besides p
toes, as I told him. The boys did not come here, as far as I
aware, to learn potato-lifting, nor have their parents expres
a particular desire to have this subject included in the c
riculum. If they had, we should very soon see it down as
Extra.

The whole thing is simply a matter of principle. If i
necessary, in the interests of discipline, to keep boys in for h
an hour after lunch, then they must be kept in. The fact t
Gilbert has put their names down for potato-lifting at that ti
is neither here nor there. He must get substitutes. Or he m
lift his infernal crop at some other time. It is absolute nonse
to say that my boys get themselves kept in on purpose to n
potato-lifting. Extra school with me is no picnic, I can ass
him.

Gilbert made me very angry by trying to argue that nothing was gained by keeping boys in, anyway. I told him, pretty sharply, to mind his own business. Let him use his own methods, and have the goodness to allow me to continue to use mine. Of course if he runs his 'Potato Gang', as he calls it, so badly that they will do anything to get out of it, that is another matter and is an additional argument for my speaking to the Head. His answer to this was that I could go and cry on the old Squid's shoulder all night for all he cared, and he hoped I should be rewarded by having the responsibility for the potatoes handed over to me. "Then,' he went on (and this is what I cannot forgive), 'when your IIIA boys bombard you with ink-pots again you can give the whole lot an extra hour on the potatoes, thus killing two birds with one stone.'

I went white with anger. Even had any ink-pots been thrown, which of course was not the case, it would have been in the worst possible taste for Gilbert to refer to it. It is an unwritten law among schoolmasters not to allude in any way to any disciplinary difficulties that a colleague may be meeting in the course of his school duties. Naturally one is aware sometimes, one cannot help being aware, that another master is failing to maintain strict order in his classroom. The noise in poor old Poole's room, towards the close of his time here, used to be indescribable. But one does *not* mention it, least of all to the man himself. Gilbert, in his proper senses, knows this as well as I do, just as he knows that it is nonsense to suggest that I, of all people, would allow ink-pots to be thrown about in my room. The fact is, he had lost his temper and was trying to make capital out of an accident that happened yesterday morning in my Algebra period — an accident that happened, moreover, *after* I had been obliged to tell the boys to come in for half an hour after lunch, and so had nothing to do with their punishment at all.

I kept them in, as a matter of fact, because they were rather silly and over-excited about taking out some brackets. I was showing them that the way to get rid of the brackets in an expression like $(a+b)(a-b)$ was to multiply out, resulting in $a^2 - b^2$, when Mason, who is rather a thorn in my side in some ways, objected that in the previous Algebra period we had started with $a^2 - b^2$ and got it to $(a+b)(a-b)$.

'Yes, Mason?' I said, not quite understanding what he was driving at.

'Well, sir, now we have started with $(a+b)(a-b)$ and got it to $a^2 - b^2$.'

'Exactly. That shows we were right yesterday, doesn't it?'

'Yes, sir, but there doesn't seem any end to it. When it's $a^2 - b^2$ we have to work away and get it to $(a+b)(a-b)$ and when it is $(a+b)(a-b)$ you're still not satisfied, sir, and we have all the trouble of making it into $a^2 - b^2$ again, sir. Couldn't we jolly well make up our minds which is best and leave it alone, sir?'

Another boy shouted, 'It's not fair, sir,' and in a moment the whole set was talking at once, urging me to 'make up my mind' and 'leave well alone', and a lot more extravagant nonsense. One boy even had the impertinence to offer odds of three to one on $a^2 - b^2$.

When the whole form forgets itself, it is worse than useless to try to pick out particular offenders. Jump on the whole lot and teach them a good lesson. Half an hour extra does them no real harm. I used it, in this case, to explain clearly to them why it is that sometimes one wants to factorize an expression and sometimes to resolve or simplify it, taking instances from problems in real life. They rather enjoyed it, I think.

In any case, all this had nothing whatever to do with the ink-pots which Gilbert saw on the floor round my desk when he looked in to borrow my dictionary at the end of the period. I had thrown them there myself, if he only knew – for reasons I may jot down here later on, but which I certainly do not feel called upon to explain to him.

We are not on speaking terms at present, which I always think a pity on a small staff, particularly as Miss Coombes – however, there is no need to go into that now.

FRIDAY

Gilbert and Rawlinson were talking about discipline in the Common Room the other day, when we were all hanging up our gowns after morning school, and Rawlinson suddenly said, 'You'd better ask A.J. about that. He's the expert on lines in these parts.'

'I see nothing to laugh at in that, Rawlinson,' I said, colouring up, and I added that, although I very much disliked giving impositions, it was sometimes necessary in order to keep the boys up to concert pitch.

'Your IIIA lot were at concert pitch all right this morning,' said Gilbert. 'I heard them from the Library.'

'Anyway, Rawlinson,' I said, ignoring Gilbert, who is inclined at times to let his tongue run away with him, 'I think it better to set a few lines than to keep a whole form in on a fine afternoon, as some people do.'

Rawlinson, knowing very well what I meant, replied that he had kept the Lower Fourth in because they seemed incapable of learning the second page of principal parts, not because they had tied his boot-laces together or put soot in his waistcoat-pockets. This silly and exaggerated reference to a forgotten incident of my apprentice-days angered me very much and I went in to lunch without another word. My temper had been a little frayed that morning by Matron in one of her fussy moods. She started some long rigmarole after Prayers about the boys' socks, and when I attempted to explain that the boys' socks had nothing whatever to do with me she became almost impertinent. 'Pardon me, Mr Wentworth,' she said, 'but the boys' socks have a great deal to do with *me*' (a thing I had never dreamed of denying), 'and I cannot possibly run my department properly without reasonable co-operation from the masters. What is the use of my laying out clean socks for the boys on Sunday morning if they are to be taken out for a walk in the afternoon through some of the muddiest places in Wilminster? The *state* that those boys' feet were in, Mr Wentworth! It's really too bad.' After some further inconclusive talk we parted, but the incident rankled. I am here to *teach*, not to trifle with hosiery.

I only mention this to explain why I was perhaps a little hasty with Rawlinson later in the day.

The talk about impositions recurred to me today when

Mason showed up fifty lines I had had to give him for makin
an uncouth noise. As he handed them in immediately aft
break and I had only set them during the first period I aske
him how he had managed to find time to do them, and h
explained that he had done them in advance at the week-en
This aroused my suspicions and I looked more closely at th
lines, only to find that they were not lines at all but some o
history notes torn bodily from an exercise-book. Mason the
said that he had done it as a protest against the system of givin
lines, which he regarded as a rotten sort of impot. Naturally n
self-respecting master can allow the boys to dictate to him th
kind of punishment they prefer, and I told Mason prett
sharply to go to his desk and sit down; but what he had said
coupled with Rawlinson's remarks, made me wonder wheth
I could not devise some more satisfactory disciplinary measur

After a little thought I hit on a plan. First I wrote down th
names of the boys on a slip of paper. Then I held this up fo
them to see and explained that I proposed to mark a cros
against the name of any boy who misbehaved in any wa
during the period. I should say nothing at the time, but if a
the end of the period any boy had three crosses against hi
name he would be severely dealt with.

'What will happen?' asked Hillman.

'Wait and see, my friend,' I replied. I had not, as a matte
of fact, made up my mind about this, but naturally I did no
let the boys know. If there is one thing that really frighten
them, it is suspense.

Clarke then asked whether a boy would only get one cros
at a time, whatever he did.

'No, Clarke,' I replied. 'I shall give *two* crosses for imperti
nence'; and I immediately made two marks against his nam
on the list.

'That's not fair, sir,' he cried. 'I didn't know we'd begun.'

I stared at him without a word until one of us was forcec
to look away.

'Do you want to have a *third* cross?' I asked quietly.

He made no reply, and I turned to Atkins, who had hi
hand up.

'May I ask a question, sir?'

'If it is a sensible one – yes,' I said, without much hope.

'I only wondered if Sapoulos gets a cross if he cries, sir.'

'Be careful, Atkins,' I warned him, taking up my pencil, and I was glad to see that there was an immediate hush. I then proceeded with the working out of some simultaneous equations on the board, and the rest of the period passed quietly enough. Once or twice I went to my desk without a word and made an ostentatious mark on the paper, but I took care not to give any boy more than two crosses. I want more time to decide what I am going to do in cases of serious disobedience.

I was still at the board when the bell rang and several of the keener boys crowded round to ask me to explain points in the working-out that they had not understood. It was some minutes before I could get to my desk to collect my books, and when I did so I noticed at once that the punishment list had been tampered with. There were six crosses against the name of every boy except that of Sapoulos, who had twelve. No doubt the boy who did this imagined I might not notice or that I might believe I had actually made all these marks myself. He will soon learn, whoever he is, that it is a bad mistake to under-rate your enemy.

I am not going to put up with this kind of thing. Tomorrow I shall tell them that they will only have themselves to thank if I go back to the old system of lines, which they appear to dislike so much. And I shall not mince my words.

SATURDAY

The whole nib question will, I think, have to be gone into rather thoroughly at our next Common Room meeting. Would it do if the boys had a box of nibs each at the beginning of term, to be kept in their desks and used as sparingly as possible on the understanding that they had to last till the end of term? C.G. says they would get through the whole lot in a fortnight. He says they use them as ballast for paper aeroplanes and so on. I know nothing about this. I don't allow paper aeroplanes, or darts for that matter, in my classroom, and what boys do in their spare time is of course no concern of mine. But I think he exaggerates. If boys are not to be trusted to look after their own nibs the school may as well close down, it seems to me. Encourage a sense of responsibility, as the Headmaster himself says, and you are half-way to the formation of real character. I believe he would be on my side in this business. The present system wastes far too much time.

This morning I was in the middle of a rather important demonstration (tangents) on the board when Hillman asked for a new nib. I told him that he did not need a nib in order to listen to a demonstration, and he replied that he would need one as soon as they started on the Riders. 'Then ask for it then,' I said. He objected that this would mean he would lose time while the others were working and would get behindhand. I saw the justice of this, but pointed out that it would have been better for everybody if he had asked for his nib at the beginning of the period instead of interrupting the lesson half-way through. He said he had only just noticed that his nib was broken; it must have got caught in the hinge of his desk while he was looking for a ruler. I might well have asked him what business he had to be looking for a ruler when he was supposed to be following my explanation on the board, but to save time I gave him a nib from the box in my desk and told him to be more careful in future.

Three more boys then came up in quick succession and asked for nibs, and as I had given one to Hillman I could not in fairness refuse them to the others. All this delay was maddening enough, but worse was to follow, for while the third boy was standing by my desk I heard a sharp cry and looked up to see Sapoulos with his head wedged in one of the lockers, while Atkins and Mason were trying to pull him out by the arms. This at any rate was the explanation given me by Mason, and I was forced to accept it, for as I stepped down from the dais I tripped somehow over my gown and fell to the floor, though not heavily, so that I was unable to see whether Sapoulos was really incapable of freeing himself or not. By the time I had recovered my feet and assured the boys who ran to my aid that I was unhurt, the incident was over and the three boys back at their desks.

Naturally I asked Sapoulos why he had gone to his locker without permission, but he was sobbing and unable to speak, and Atkins volunteered the information that Sapoulos was looking, he believed, for a pen.

I threw up my hands.

'*Where* is the boy's pen?' I demanded.

'It is in the tool-house of my gardener's aunt,' said Mason.

I never overlook impertinence, and I gave Mason a talking-to which he will, I think, remember as long as he lives. I told him that he had come to Burgrove not to be a public buffoon or to practise the art of being rude to those who were a good deal older and perhaps even a little wiser than himself, but to learn. Presumably, I said, it was the wish of his parents who were spending their money on his education that he should fit himself for a Public School and afterwards for some useful career. At present I could see no prospect of either wish being fulfilled. He would have to pull himself together and take up a very different attitude towards his school-work if he was to have the slightest chance of getting through Common Entrance; and as for a career, unless there was an unexpected demand for third-rate comedians, I could not see any way in which the world would be likely to make use of his services. There will have to be a big change, Mason,' I told him, 'or you and I will find ourselves at loggerheads.'

'*You* may,' he said. '*I'm* going to Cheltenham.'

I sent him out of the room at once, and when he had gone Clarke asked for some blotting-paper, which I refused. We masters always have enough nibs in our desk for the boys' needs, but pens and blotting-paper are kept in the stationery cupboard of which Rawlinson holds the key. This means that in order to gain access to the pens and so on, except at the stated times on Mondays, Wednesdays and Fridays when the cupboard is open, one has to send a chit for whatever one wants to Rawlinson. This I was not prepared to do merely to provide Clarke with blotting-paper, especially as every boy has a clean sheet put on his desk every Monday morning. Rawlinson is not particularly keen on receiving chits during morning school, and the row I had with him over the pegs in the changing-

room makes me chary of asking favours. So I tore my ov
blotting-paper in half and gave a piece to Clarke. He made
into a dart, which I confiscated according to my invariab
rule.

We then turned our attention to the angular relationsh
between tangents and radii.

Mason came in while I was busy with the large wood
compasses we use for work on the board and said he was sor
if he had been rude. He said he was playing for the Secor
Eleven that afternoon and was rather excited. I told him I w
glad to hear he had been chosen, but that he must try 1
remember that football was not the important thing in li
Work must come first.

This, for some reason, made all the boys laugh.

A boy called Phillips got into my bad books this afternoon.
was too wet for football after all (which was hard luck c
Mason) so we all put on our macs and went for a walk, Gilbe
taking the Seniors round by Fotherham Dyke, while tl
Juniors came with me for a ramble in Marling Wood
Sapoulos and young Hopgood asked if they might walk wit
me and I consented, since I like to give this privilege to all th
boys in turn, and Hillman, who also asked, had the position o
my right as recently as three weeks ago. I always make a not
of these things; boys are so quick to notice any unfairness c
favouritism.

Well, I was talking to Hopgood about footer when a bo
came running back to say that Phillips was stuck in a drai
and couldn't move. (I say running *back* because of course w
masters always keep behind when taking a walk; it is the bes
place to keep an eye on the boys, see that they are wearin
their caps properly and so on. The young rascals take them of
and put them in their pockets if they get half a chance, whicl
is against the School rules.)

'Phillips has no business to be in a drain at all, as you know
perfectly well, Clarke,' I said brusquely; but none the less
hurried off after him as fast as I could.

We found the whole walk collected at a point where a

shallow but muddy stream runs under the path through a
circular drain or culvert some twelve to fifteen feet in length.
I at once ordered the boys to stand away from all that mud
and, pushing them aside, lowered myself cautiously to the level
of the water. Then, clinging with my left hand to a convenient
stump of wood, I bent down and peered into the drain. I could
see nothing at all owing to the darkness, so I said, 'Come out of
here at once, Phillips, d'you hear?' It had struck me immediately that he might very well be playing the fool and merely
pretending to be stuck. However, there was no reply, and I
repeated the order in a louder tone.

'Perhaps he'd hear better if you went round to the other
end, sir,' suggested Mason, who was watching from the other
side of the stream. 'His head's facing that way.'

'Just *look* at your boots, Mason!' I cried. 'Whatever will
Matron say?'

I did not catch his reply, for at this moment the stump unluckily gave way and I was precipitated into the water. Instinctively I thrust out both hands as I fell, but, remembering my
wrist-watch just in time, drew back my right arm without
realizing that this would inevitably throw me forwards on my
head. As it turned out I rolled completely over and thus failed
after all to save the watch from a ducking. But by a miracle I
kept my wallet dry.

'What did you say, Mason?' I asked as I rose.

'Nothing, sir.'

This I knew to be an untruth, but in the circumstances it
seemed best to pass it over. Accordingly I showed my dis-
pleasure only by a look and, scrambling up the bank, made my
way through a crowd of gaping boys to the other end of the
culvert. Here there was no difficulty, for the bank was less
steep and, my boots being already full of water, I was able to
stand boldly in midstream. Almost at once I made out the
white glimmer of Phillips' face just beyond a kind of iron
grating which must no doubt have arrested his progress.

'Is that you, Phillips?' I asked.

'Yes, sir.'

'May I ask what you think you are doing in there?'

'I'm stuck, sir.'

'Possibly,' I said. 'Where are you stuck?'

'At the back, sir. My coat got rucked up when I tried to g
back, sir, and I think – I'm not sure, sir, but I think my brace
are caught on the roof, sir.'

'Are your feet wet?'

'A bit, sir.'

'Tut!' I said. 'This is a bad business, Phillips. How lon
have you been here?'

'About five minutes, sir.'

'Don't be ridiculous, boy!' I said angrily. 'I mean how lon
have you been at the School?'

'Oh, four terms, sir.'

'Quite long enough to know better,' I said sternly, and tol
him to stay where he was until he was released.

I then called the boys to me and told them that Phillips wa
caught by his braces at the back, and as his feet were wet h
must be got out at once or there might be serious consequence
I explained that I was too large to enter the drain, and tha
one of them must therefore volunteer to crawl in at the en
where – at the end which I had first investigated, and attemp
to free Phillips' braces.

'Can I do it, sir?'

'Very well, Mason,' I said, 'but take off your shoes an
stockings and roll up your trousers. I cannot have the whol
Junior School soaking wet.'

It was an anxious time for us all while Mason was in th
drain, but eventually he reappeared and clambered up th
bank.

'Well, Mason?' I cried eagerly.

'I've freed his braces, sir,' he cried, holding them up.

'Mason,' I said in my coldest voice. 'This is no time fo
joking. Where is Phillips?'

'In the drain, sir. He daren't come out.'

Mason explained that Phillips had decided to stay in th
drain because he was afraid of being punished when he cam
out. He said – Mason said, that is – that he thought if Phillips

ew for certain nothing would happen to him he would come
at once.

'Did you suggest this to him, Mason?' I asked sternly.

'Me, sir? Good lord, no sir!'

'Tell him to come out this instant,' I cried, losing all patience
h the lot of them, 'or I'll report him to the Headmaster for
hrashing.'

When Phillips came out and I saw the state of his clothes
d the muddy boots of the other boys into the bargain I was
despair.

'I'd like to know what Matron will have to say about this,'
aid, half to myself.

Mason, who can never learn to mind his own business,
pped in at once. 'Wouldn't it be easiest, sir,' he suggested,
explain that you fell into the stream and we all got a bit
ty helping you out?'

'Very easy indeed, Mason,' I replied sarcastically, 'if you
think of any reason why I *should* have fallen into the
eam.'

'Need there be a special reason, sir?'

'Am I the kind of person who goes about falling into streams
no reason whatever?' I asked.

'We – ell . . .' said Mason.

I gave him a thundering good wigging for that piece of
pertinence.

NDAY

ease, sir, how do you spell "codger"?'

Among the tasks of the master on duty on Sundays is invigi-
ion during the boys' letter-writing hour after morning
apel; though invigilation is not the right word perhaps, since
e does not have to look out for cribbing or anything of that
t. One is there to help and to see that the boys keep quiet
d get on with their letters. Naturally, if there was any crib-
ng, I mean if one boy was leaning over to see what the next
y was writing, one would put a stop to it, because they ought
be able to think of something to say to their parents on their
n. Besides, we believe in the boys' correspondence being

absolutely private – letters are not read and censored here
any of that nonsense, I am glad to say.

The boy who asked me to help with his spelling was you
Fraser (red hair and freckles) and for a moment I failed
follow him. ' "Codger", Fraser?' I repeated. 'What sort
codger?'

'Silly old codger,' said Mason.

There was nothing to get hold of about that, really, thou
I half suspected impertinence. 'Well, Fraser?' I remark
brushing Mason's interruption aside. 'Do you particula
want to use that word? Not that there's anything against it
added with a smile, 'except that it's slang, of course, a
rather old-fashioned slang at that.'

Some silly boy asked whether 'Geezer' would be more
to date, but I signalled to him to be quiet, and to save furtl
argument spelled out Fraser's word. I had just returned to :
book, a most interesting biography of Gustavus Adolph
about whom I have often wondered, when another boy asl
me how to spell 'coot'.

I looked up to find the whole school watching me.

'Get on, get on, you others,' I warned them. 'Are you writi
nature notes, Parkinson?'

He said he was not, going rather red in the face for so
reason.

'But, all the same, you wish to tell your parents somethi
about coots, is that it?'

'Only about one, sir.'

'I see,' I said. 'A particular coot. What is there funny
that, Mason?'

'Nothing, sir.'

'Then why laugh?'

'I don't know, sir. Sir, are they really mad as well as ba
sir?'

'Stop this silly laughter immediately,' I cried, and almost
once the hubbub died down. To my surprise Mason persist
with his question, which I had not been intending to ta
seriously.

'Sir, why *do* people say he's as mad as a coot, sir?' he asked. 't's an awfully funny sort of thing to say, isn't it, sir?'

'Sir, there's a book about a pig,' began Tremayne excitedly e is not one of my IIA boys, of course), but I cut him short. That will do, all of you,' I said sharply. 'Sensible questions are ne thing, but we cannot spend the whole hour discussing the abits of coots. Or pigs either,' I added, with a glance at remayne. 'It's twenty past already.'

When Pettigrew asked me how many bats there were in elfry' I decided the thing was getting beyond a joke. 'No ore questions for ten minutes,' I ordered. 'Any boy who is in ifficulties can come up to my desk at the end of that time and sk me quietly.'

Quite a number of boys came up when the ten minutes were ver, and I was explaining to de Groot about postal rates to Iolland (a schoolmaster has to be an expert on a hundred and ne things nowadays. Goodness knows what poor old Poole ould have made of it all – he was French master here for a umber of years until the boys put salt in his hair. There were ne or two other contretemps as a matter of fact; the Head- aster might have overlooked an isolated incident). Well, I as talking to de Groot, as I was saying, when an infernal hindy broke out about half-way down the queue.

'Stop that scrimmaging about there,' I shouted. 'Fraser, hat are you doing?'

'Somebody hacked me on the heel, sir.'

'Sneak,' said Mason.

'It isn't sneaking to say "somebody".'

'Oh, no! Considering nobody could have hacked you xcept the next man in the queue.'

'You're sneaking yourself now,' said Fraser.

I put my spectacles down firmly on the desk and rose to my eet.

'Go to your desks all of you,' I said quietly. 'I will not have his ridiculous arguing and bickering during Letter-Hour. You an all just get on with it straight away without any more fuss. And *stop* fiddling with that watch, Jenkins. You've written ractically nothing.'

Jenkins is a new boy, who probably hasn't had a watch of his own before, but all the same he has been here long enough now to know that he must not fiddle with it in class, or in Letter-Hour, which comes to the same thing. He told me feebly, that he didn't know what to say.

'My dear boy,' I replied. 'Surely you can write your own letters home. This is not supposed to be Dictation period. Tell them what you did last week. Tell them what is going to happen next week, if you like.'

'*Is* anything going to happen next week?' asked Mason.

I always try to avoid sarcasm, but this was too much. 'Considering the School plays Fox House away on Wednesday and on Thursday there is a lecture on the Ice Age – '

'With slides?' asked some fool.

' – and the second monthly form-order will be out at the week-end, even you, Mason,' I continued smoothly, 'can hardly regard next week as a complete blank. What boy interrupted me just now?'

Nobody owned up, so I put on a Silence rule. 'Anybody who speaks in this room without my permission,' I told them 'will get a hundred lines.' You could have heard a pin drop. I did hear a nib, as a matter of fact – Mason of course. But I had my eye on him, and he bent down and picked it up without a word. Then, as ill-luck would have it, Miss Coombes came in with some music lists.

'Oh, Mr Wentworth,' she began, but the rest of the sentence was lost in a gale of laughter in which, I am ashamed to say, I could not refrain from joining. Somehow the idea of coming down on poor Miss Coombes with a hefty impot was irresistibly comic.

She went very red in the face and marched out without another word, not understanding the joke, of course. I am afraid she will be upset, though I shall make a point of explaining things to her after lunch, naturally.

The absurd incident had one good effect, for the boys settled down straight away, everybody scribbling away quite contentedly for the rest of the hour. I had my suspicions of what they were all writing about – suspicions which were pretty well

firmed when, right at the end, Fraser asked me how to spell
embarrassed.

'Two "r's", Fraser,' I told him, and was unable to resist
adding, 'The "ass", no doubt you are familiar with?'

The boys were quick to appreciate my little dig at him and
everybody laughed. They laughed still more when Fraser
replied, 'Yes, thank you, sir. I've got him down already,'
though I confess I failed to see the point.

Anyway, I hope they won't say anything derogatory about
Miss Coombes in their letters. She is a friendly soul, though
inclined to be a little weak – of which the boys, I have reason
to think, sometimes take advantage.

Lent Term 1939
The Man Faggott

SATURDAY, 21 JANUARY

After the bustle and excitement of the first day of term it w
a real shock to me to be informed quite casually by Gilbert t
morning that he is taking over eleven o'clock milkers. Elev
o'clock milkers is our name here for the distribution of n
during break to certain boys whose parents have expresse
wish that they should have it, and for years it has been
prerogative to tick off the names of these boys as they come
for their glasses. The last thought in my mind as I ente
Common Room after breakfast was that any change could
contemplated in this arrangement – certainly not without c
sulting me.

Of course I went straight off to the Headmaster the mom
I heard of it.

I found him interviewing some parents who had brou
their boy, a new boy, down a day late, and would have w
drawn at once, but Mr Saunders beckoned me in.

'Ah, Wentworth!' he cried, 'I'm glad you looked in.
Wentworth is one of our little community of assistant mast
Mrs Carter – a very happy little community, eh, Wentwort
I'm sure he will help Johnny all he can.'

'How do you do, Mrs Carter?' I said. 'We will certainly
our best to put young Johnny on the right road. You need ha
no doubt that he will be happy here at Burgrove – and w
hard, won't you, Johnny?'

The little boy made no reply, and I turned to his father.

'Why, Mr Carter,' I exclaimed admiringly, 'he's the livi
image of you!'

'I should have introduced you,' put in Mrs Carter, colouring prettily. 'This is Captain Ferguson, a very kind friend who motored us down.'

It would have been the work of a moment to cover up this little misunderstanding, but in stepping backwards to address a remark about the mild weather to Mrs Carter I had the misfortune to tread on her boy's foot; he had somehow got round behind me in that irritating way young people have. Naturally I apologized, but he burst into tears, and indeed made a most unnecessary fuss about the incident.

'Come, come, Johnny,' I said kindly. 'You are a big boy now. You must learn to put up with a few hard knocks now you have come to Burgrove.'

'Why is that, Mr Wentworth?' cried his mother, mistaking my meaning. 'Do you make a point of treading on the boys' feet at this school?'

'No, Mrs Carter,' I replied, turning the point neatly though perfectly politely, against her. 'We teach the boys to stand on their *own* feet at Burgrove.'

'Well, Wentworth,' said the Headmaster, rather shortly for him, 'is there anything you want to see me about?'

'Nothing that will not keep until you are free, thank you, Headmaster,' I replied, and with a smile that included them all I turned on my heel and walked into a maidenhair fern which Mr Saunders, rashly as I think, keeps on a tall stand by the door. Only great quickness on my part saved the pot from falling to the floor, and finding myself with the fern in my arms I decided that the best thing to do was to walk straight out with it, pretending that I had meant all along to take it with me. This naturally made it impossible for me to shut the door, and thus as I walked through the swing-door into the boys' part of the house I overheard Mrs Carter make a remark which I greatly resented. Nothing is to be gained by repeating it here.

I had a busy day and had almost forgotten the trifling annoyances of the morning, when the Headmaster summoned me to his study.

'Well, Wentworth,' he began, 'have you any explanation to offer?'

'Explanation?' I stammered.

'Of your rudeness to one of our parents and your extraordinary action in removing an ornament from my room without permission and without explanation of any kind?'

'If you are referring to the maidenhair fern,' I replied, controlling myself with difficulty, 'I can only say that I should have thought my reasons for taking it were obvious.'

'Not to me,' he said, and added that even if he could conceive some object for which a fern was necessary in my day's work, as for example to illustrate some scientific point to the boys or as a drawing model – though it would be news to him to learn that I was concerned with the teaching either of science or drawing at Burgrove, even so he still could not imagine that the need was of such urgency as to justify the methods I had adopted to acquire one. He had heard, he went on, of men subject to sudden ungovernable impulses which made the possession of some desired object a paramount consideration, but if that was the explanation he only wished I had given him some inkling of my desire for a maidenhair fern. He could then have had one placed in my room at the beginning of term and this deplorable incident would have been avoided. But on the whole, he said, he preferred to think that my action was simply a particularly mistaken and ill-timed piece of clowning.

'If that is what you think, Headmaster,' I burst out at last, 'I have no option but to resign my position here. I have spent many happy, and I like to think not unproductive, years at Burgrove, and I shall be sorry, more than sorry, to go – '

'We shall be sorry to lose you, Wentworth.'

'There is no reason why you *should* lose me,' I rejoined warmly. 'The whole ridiculous incident has been magnified out of all proportion. I will go and fetch this precious fern *now*. That I should be accused at my age of kleptomania and – and clownishness – is incredible!'

Blind with rage I turned to the door, but as ill luck would have it, caught my foot against the fern-stand and went down heavily against a table of silver spoons and other small bric-à-

ac. When I rose to my feet, still automatically clutching the
and, there were tears of mortification in my eyes.

'Headmaster – ' I began.

'Leave me the stand, Wentworth,' he cried, 'at least leave
e the stand!' and to my amazement I saw that he was
ailing.

I would have spoken, but he checked me with a gesture.

'Never mind about it now,' he said. 'We'll talk about it later.
ad let me have my fern back when you've finished with it,
on't you?'

I said good night, and as I walked away an explosion of
aughter followed me down the corridor. I went to my room
write up this diary with my mind in a whirl.

EDNESDAY, I FEBRUARY

*he following account of an incident, not mentioned in Mr
'entworth's diary, has been sent to me by Mr Charles Gilbert,
ne of his colleagues. It sheds a certain light on some of the
tfalls of the profession.]*

I hear that old ass Wentworth has been sending you extracts
om his precious diary, though what he hopes to gain by it
oodness only knows. But I don't suppose for a moment he has
aade any mention of the great Night Alarm – one of his finest
xploits, and I thought you might like to know about it.

Well, one night I was sitting in my room down at the
Iasters' Cottage taking my boots off and fearing no evil, when
heard a great disturbance next door, and in a moment Went-
orth came tearing in with an incoherent story about not being
ble to get into bed and how he'd make trouble for Mrs Barnett
ver this in the morning. I went along with him to investigate
nd, as I'd rather expected, found he'd got an apple-pie bed.
s I say, I wasn't surprised because as a matter of fact I'd made
myself, but what did astonish me was that Wentworth
bviously didn't know what it was. That's the trouble with
im. You never can gauge the depths of the man's simplicity.
Ie seemed to think that Mrs Barnett, who does for us at the
ottage, had made a hash of her job when she made up the
ed, and he was absolutely set on putting her through it for

what he called her 'abominable carelessness'. Naturally
didn't want Mrs Barnett to be unjustly accused, so I explain
that sometimes people went into other people's rooms a
turned up the bottom sheet in this way simply in order
surprise the owner of the room when he went to bed. 'Just a
joke,' I added.

'But who could have done such a senseless thing?' he aske

He looked quite upset about it, so I shook my head. But
thought there was no harm in mentioning that I'd se
Collingridge hanging about the cottage just after dinner.

'Collingridge!' said Wentworth. 'I thought he had mo
sense.' You could see the idea came as quite a shock to him, b
after a while I persuaded him that the only way to settle it w
to go straight up to Collingridge's room and tax him with
'Pull the bedclothes off him, A.J.,' I said. 'Then he'll leave yo
alone in future.'

In the end he put some clothes on and set off. Collingrid,
sleeps up at the school, because there's no room in the cottag
and my idea was that he'd just about have had time to cle
out the holly I'd put in his bed and get settled down for t
night before Wentworth arrived. Then if Wentworth took n
advice and whipped the clothes off him I thought there mig
possibly be some fun. . . .

The last thing I expected to hear was the fire-alarm goin

What happened apparently was this. Wentworth, with h
peculiar genius for taking the wrong turning and a good de
aided by the fact that all the lights in the school corridors a
switched off at half-past ten, went slap into Matron's roon
which lies relatively in the same position on the right at the to
of the main stairs as Collingridge's room does on the left. H
got out again, he says, before she got to the light-switch, but he
screams must have upset him because he ran too much to th
right and came a most frightful purler over a row of enam
water-jugs they put out along the wall of the corridor ready fo
the morning. Well, you know the kind of noise a lot of empt
enamelware makes when you start it rolling about the floor an
down the stairs. Wentworth, I should imagine lost his nerv

altogether, and it must have been more luck than judgement that made him bolt into Collingridge's room.

Collingridge, who had had about enough of all this disturbance, hit him a tremendous wallop with a pillow just as Matron set the fire alarm going.

I'm told there was a fair amount of pandemonium. The rule is that on hearing the alarm at night all boys are to put on their dressing-gowns and proceed in an orderly manner to the gymnasium – unless, I suppose, the gymnasium happens to be on fire; but I don't believe there's any provision for that. All I know is that when I got to the gym everybody seemed to be talking at once, and in the middle of it Matron was trying to explain to the Headmaster, who looks a good deal less impressive in a check dressing-gown, that there wasn't any fire but that somebody, or so she thought – though she might have been mistaken – had attempted to get into her bedroom. ('Get back to your dormitories, all you boys,' said the Reverend Saunders at this point.) Anyway, what *had* alarmed her and made her feel it was her duty, to the boys if not to herself, to ring the alarm, was a terrible noise as if some kind of wild beast were crashing and rolling about among the hot-water jugs in the corridor.

The moment old Saunders heard this about the jugs he began to look round for Wentworth. The fact is that whenever you hear a loud crash at Burgrove or see a pile of play-boxes or bowler-hats toppling to the ground you instinctively expect to catch sight of Wentworth making an unobtrusive disappearance round a corner, and you are very rarely disappointed. Wentworth wasn't in the gym, as he should have been after a fire-alarm, and I thought it only right to point out that Collingridge wasn't there either. 'No doubt,' I said, 'there is some perfectly good reason for their absence.'

There was. It became painfully clear, to me at least, what was detaining them as soon as we reached the top of the main stairs, but to the others I dare say the thudding sounds that came from the direction of Collingridge's room only made the mystery more mysterious.

'Odd!' said the Headmaster, pausing. 'Very odd. Do you think I should go in?'

For myself, I thought it far better that he shouldn't, but on the spur of the moment I could think of no argument to support this view. So I nodded dumbly and followed him in.

What old Saunders expected to see I have no idea, but I am pretty certain that it never struck him he might be intruding on a death-grapple between two of his assistant-masters. The room was a shambles, but it was the combatants who took the eye. At the moment of our entry they had got themselves into a corner beyond the bed, where Collingridge, with his head in Wentworth's stomach, was trying with a conscientiousness one could not help admiring to thrust him into a cupboard obviously two or three sizes too small for him. Wentworth, a good deal handicapped by having a sheet over his head and both feet practically off the ground, was contenting himself with belabouring his opponent's back with his fists, but I must say he was making a sound job of it.

'*Get* in there, can't you?' Collingridge was saying, butting hard.

'Ouch!' said Wentworth.

'*Wentworth*!' cried the Headmaster in an awful voice. 'Are you mad?'

The question that so many have asked themselves at various stages of Wentworth's career might have been answered then and there if only the old boy hadn't been too short of wind and too much bothered by the sheet to reply. While they were getting themselves disentangled and Wentworth was doing his bashful utmost to scrape the cupboard off his back, I took my leave. I thought that they could probably explain the whole thing between them without any help from me.

But, as I told Wentworth next morning, he'll really have to learn to control his passions a bit better or he'll be getting the sack. Of course I was referring to his scrap with Collingridge, but for some reason of his own he chose to think I meant the Matron. You never saw a man in such a lather.

[*This concludes Mr Gilbert's narrative.*]

TUESDAY, 14 FEBRUARY

People ask me sometimes whether I find the schoolboy of today noticeably quieter and more mature than his elder brother of, say, the early thirties. I cannot see it. I detect precious little difference in the young rascals. More knowledgeable perhaps on some subjects, aircraft modelling to take an obvious instance, but as bone-headed as ever over the important things. I can still twist their tails with a simultaneous quadratic; and it is still just as difficult to make them see that unless they stick to a problem, really worry at it, for themselves, instead of throwing up their hands and shouting 'Sir, Sir,' at the slightest set-back, they will never make mathematicians.

And the *time* we waste. Yesterday, after break, I told Set IIIA to write down one third as a decimal.

'Everybody finished?' I asked.

'No, sir,' said Mason.

I gave him another half-minute and then told him to stop.

'But it *won't* stop, sir.'

Everybody laughed.

'I mean it goes on and on, sir, and if I stop before it does my answer won't be right.'

'What have you got, Mason?'

'Well, sir, so far I've got point three three three three three three three three three three three three three three three three – that's correct to sixteen decimal places, sir.'

'There's nothing to laugh about!' I said sharply. 'What have you got there, Atkins?'

'Me, sir? Point three recurring, sir.'

'I am not asking for the answer to the sum. I am asking you what you have got in your right hand.'

'Nothing, sir.'

Boys invariably try this answer first, though they must know they have precious little chance of getting away with it with an old hand like me. Atkins had that boiled look that tells you at once when a boy is caught out.

'Bring it up here, Atkins,' I said. 'And the rest of you express point seven three five as a fraction.'

I wrote it up on the board to stop endless questions and then took the piece of paper Atkins handed to me.

He had simply scribbled the headmaster's name, 'Rev Gregory Saunders, M.A.', on the paper, and I was about to send him back to his desk with a caution against wasting the time of the form when I noticed that the paper was folded over at the bottom.

'An old dodge, Atkins,' I said, unfolding it.

He had written 'The Beast of Burgrove' under the head-master's name, a serious offence.

'I can't possibly overlook this, Atkins,' I told him sternly.

'Couldn't you overlook it on his birthday, sir?' asked Mason.

'Is it your birthday, Atkins?' I asked.

'No, sir.'

'In that case, Mason, I fail to see the point of your remark. Even if it was any business of yours – '

'I was only wondering, sir, whether if it *had* been his birth-day, it would have made any difference.'

'Mason!' I warned him. 'That will do. When I want your advice about the way to treat people on their birthday, I will ask for it. Birthdays make no difference to the fact that we've all come here to work, and the sooner everyone realizes that the better.'

'Is it your birthday, sir?' somebody called out, and there was an immediate chorus of cries from the other boys. 'Jolly good, Duce,' 'Wake up, Duce,' 'Have some macaroni, Benito,' and a lot more nonsense of the same kind, which I very soon stamped on. Benito is not the boy's real name, of course (though we have quite a number of French and Belgians here now, besides Sapoulos, the Greek; and a little Dutch boy called de Groot came last term); but the others call him that because of some fancied resemblance to the Italian leader.

'Now then,' I said. 'Let's see who's got this fraction right. Otterway?'

'Not quite ready yet, sir.'

'Hurry up, boy. Trench?'

'Well, sir, I've done it, only it seems rather an absurd answer.'

'Never mind that,' I said. 'I'm used to absurd answers. What is it?'

'A hundred and forty-seven over two hundred.'

'What's absurd about that? Well, Williamson?'

'I thought I heard the bell, sir.'

I slammed my book down on the desk.

'If you would kindly attend to your work, instead of listening for the school bell, we might conceivably get through a fraction of what we have to do before the end of term – perhaps even a hundred and forty-seven two hundredths of it, Trench.'

'Jolly good, sir!' said Mason.

I told them they might go, and began to collect my things for my English period.

'May I go too, sir?' asked Atkins, about whom, I am bound to confess, I had rather forgotten.

I took up a piece of chalk and tossed it in the air.

'What are we going to do about this, Atkins?' I said. 'Eh?'

'I don't know, sir. I'm sorry, sir.'

'H'm!' I said, not knowing either. 'I'll have to think about it.'

I shall probably decide to do nothing in the end. The boy has had a good fright, which is the main thing.

WEDNESDAY, 1 MARCH

Rawlinson is down with flu and a man called Faggott has come in for a week or two. He is a Major apparently – one of those stocky red-faced men with a moustache which sprouts out in a disagreeable way over uneven yellow teeth. He whistles too, and is – well, more abrupt in manner towards some of the regular staff than one altogether expects or relishes. No doubt it is difficult to get the right type of man for such a short appointment, but still – there are agencies and so on which cater for this kind of emergency. One wonders if he has had much experience really; and I'm bound to say the one place one does hear of his having been at doesn't seem to me to be quite – though it's easy enough to get a false impression of these things. 'Not the way we used to do things at Marston House' – if he's said that once in the last three days he's said it a hundred times. As if we cared how they choose to do things at some potty little seaside school or other. 'All I can say is,' I remarked at last, goaded beyond endurance by some petty criticism of one of our school rules – he had chosen to be offensive, if I remember rightly, because the boys here line up in their school order when the bell rings for meals and march to their places in an orderly fashion (a thoroughly wise arrangement, as it happens) – 'All I can say is,' I remarked, 'if that's not the way you used to do it at Marston House, so much the worse for Marston House'; and I walked straight in to my place at Gainsborough (each table in the dining-room is known by the name of a famous artist or soldier – another old custom that Faggott has not hesitated to make the subject of his stupid pleasantries) without giving him a chance to reply. I was thoroughly angry.

Then this morning I told him in a perfectly friendly way that the Headmaster did not expect to see masters smoking in the school corridors or classrooms, though of course it was quite all right in Common Room. 'Rats to that!' he said, and strolled off down the passage with his foul, stumpy little pipe clamped firmly between his teeth. What can one do with such a fellow?

It is worse down at the Cottage. This evening he came barging into my room with a bottle of whisky in his hand looking for soda. 'This chap Rawlinson doesn't seem to have any in his room,' he said. Rawlinson is in the San, so Faggott has been given his room. It was on the tip of my tongue to say that Rawlinson had probably locked up his soda, and would, no doubt, if he had known who was to take his place, have locked up his whisky as well; but instead I merely replied that I had no soda to offer him and went quietly on with my correction of IIIA's work. I had a great deal to do and my manner ought to have made it clear to anyone that I was busy and wished to be left alone. But a nod is as good as a wink to a blind horse. Major Faggott wandered about the room, whistling between his teeth, examining my belongings in the coolest possible fashion, picking up a book here and a book there and laying it down again with a groan, pausing with sharp exclamations of disgust in front of my Van Gogh repro-

ductions and my college groups, going so far even as to take
up a photograph of my sister from the mantelpiece and replace
it without comment behind the ormolu clock.

'Well,' I said at last when I could stand it no longer, 'you
don't appear to have much work to do.'

He came and leaned over my shoulder. ' 'Ullo, 'ullo!' he
said, draggling his pipe-stem over the papers. 'Those curly
brackets ought to have been taken out, or I'm a Dutchman.
Three out of five.'

'Are you a mathematician, Major Faggott?'

'Me!' he said. 'You've heard of the Binomial Theorem?'

'I should hope so,' I said stiffly.

'Well, I invented it.'

'Indeed!' I said, making no attempt to keep the contempt
out of my voice. 'I was under the impression that it was
invented by Omar Khayyám.'

He roared with laughter. 'What a queer old buffer it is!
Haven't you ever read the *Rubaiyat*?'

'I have,' I answered. 'I have also read *Alice in Wonderland*.
It is quite possible for a man to be a writer as well as a mathematician — just as it should be possible for a man to be a gentleman as well as a schoolmaster.'

'It isn't,' he said, quite failing to see the implication of my
remark; 'that's why I've practically given up schoolmastering.'

I made no reply, contenting myself with ostentatiously
marking my papers, and there was silence for a long time, so
that I began to hope the man had gone. But when at last I
turned round in my chair I saw him still fiddling with the
things on my mantelpiece.

'No photograph of the Matron, I see,' he said with an
unpleasant grin.

I rose to my feet and demanded to know what he meant by
that remark. He then made a suggestion so offensive that for a
moment I was unable to speak, while the hot blood mounted
to my cheeks. Never in all my years at Burgrove have I been
spoken to in such a way — and by such a preposterous bounder.
It is typical of the man that he misinterpreted my natural flush
of indignation and was pleased to describe it as a 'guilty blush'.

I believe I might have struck him where he stood, but fortunately he saw that I was in a dangerous mood and decided to take his leave.

'Well,' he said with an attempt at nonchalance, 'if you've no soda in this rat-trap I may as well be pushing along,' and he swaggered off, turning a photograph of my old College Eight to the wall as he went out.

I went straight along to Gilbert's room as soon as he had gone. The fact is that that reference of Faggott's to a silly incident of a few weeks ago was the last straw. The whole thing was too childish. I simply tripped up in the dark one night when I was on my way to ask Collingridge about something or other, and Matron, whose room is not far away, was frightened by the noise and rang the fire-alarm. Some silly fool has exaggerated the story and told it to this impossible Faggott, who is not above twisting the whole thing round to suit his own purposes and make me look ridiculous, or worse. So I have put the whole position before Gilbert and he agrees that something must be done to put the Major – if he is a Major, which I begin to doubt – in his place. We have a sort of a plan which we think may make it clear to the Headmaster that Faggott is not at all the type for a school of this sort. Better have nobody at all until Rawlinson comes back, as I said to Gilbert, than allow a mischief-maker like Faggott the run of the place for another fortnight. I could take Rawlinson's lot with my own, if it comes to that. The desks from both classrooms would have to be moved into the gym, I suppose, though that might interfere with the Sergeant's fencing-classes. Still, fencing isn't everything.

Gilbert approved of my gym plan when I told him of it and suggested I might invigilate from the vaulting-horse – but I don't think he was serious.

MONDAY, 6 MARCH

The man Faggott continues to be a thorn in my side. Naturally as the next senior master I expected to be put in charge of the stationery cupboard during Rawlinson's absence; but Faggott, so he says, was definitely instructed by the Headmaster when he took up his temporary position here to perform all Rawlinson's duties as far as possible, and it is typical of the man's dog-in-the-manger attitude that he insists on interpreting the phrase to cover the supervision of stationery, despite his obvious lack of experience at work of this kind. This morning being Monday the cupboard was open from 9.0 to 9.30, and I thought it best to keep an eye on Faggott while the boys were coming up in turn for their requirements. As I expected, it was not long before I saw him handing out some of the special pink blotting-paper which is kept for Common Room use.

I thought it my duty to step forward and put him right at once, though I was careful to speak in a low voice in order not to discredit him in front of the boys.

'White blotting-paper?' he said, affecting to misunderstand me, and he handed me a couple of sheets without troubling to turn round.

'I do not require blotting-paper, thank you,' I said curtly.

'You soak it up yourself, eh?' he replied, accompanying this meaningless remark with a wink which made my temper rise at once. But in view of the presence of a number of boys I controlled myself and merely said it was good news to hear Rawlinson would be up again in a day or two. I think he knew what I meant.

After this it was particularly galling to hear his praises sung so loudly by IIIA during the first period after break. Apparently he has been currying favour with the boys by means of a certain facility he has for mechanical repairs, and also (and less surprisingly to those who know him) by boasting of his exploits in the Great War. Boys are extraordinarily easily taken in by men of his — I had almost said 'flashy' — type. As a result I was obliged to listen to a long account from Atkins of how Faggott had tunnelled his way out of a German fortress with a pen-knife, or some such nonsense, and when that was over Mason showed me a watch he had mended, and Hillman brought up a mechanical crane which had been newly soldered — not too well, in my opinion, though I am no artisan — just above the base. I told Hillman, rather abruptly, for I was getting tired of all this, that the classroom was no place for cranes, and a voice immediately said, 'Or pigeons' – an impertinent reference, or so I took it, to an occasion last term when a pigeon mysteriously flew out of my desk.

'Stand up the boy who said that!' I cried, and to my surprise the whole class rose to their feet. However, I am too old a hand not to recognize a concerted attempt at ragging when I see it, and I promptly decided to play them at their own game and beat them at it.

'You all said it?' I asked, only slightly raising my eyebrows. 'Very well, then, you will all be punished. A hundred lines each by tomorrow morning.'

There was a chorus of 'Oh, sirs!' which I immediately suppressed by a threat to double the imposition, and Mason then asked whether Sapoulos had to do the lines as well. I had failed to notice that the little Greek boy had remained sitting while the others got up, and my suspicions were immediately aroused.

'Did you say it, Sapoulos?' I asked sternly.

'I beg to be excused, sir,' he replied.

There was a general laugh at his quaint English, but knowing that he meant to say, 'I beg your pardon?' I repeated my question: 'Did you say "Or pigeons"?'

' "Orpigeons", sir?'

'You heard what I said.'

Sapoulos, instead of replying, kept repeating 'orpigeons, orpigeons, orpigeons' over to himself in a puzzled tone until I lost all patience with the boy.

'Sapoulos!' I thundered, 'did you or did you not say "Or pigeons"?'

The silly boy, as I feared, now began to cry, and Mason volunteered the opinion that he probably thought 'or pigeons' was one word and didn't know what it meant. I told him that when I wanted his advice I would ask for it, and added that as nearly half the period had already been wasted we should not do mental arithmetic, as I had promised, but instead would refresh our memories of Pythagoras. 'And stop that groaning,' I added sharply.

I had barely completed the construction on the blackboard

en some boy – Mason again, I think – calmly announced,
thout even troubling to hold up his hand: 'Major Faggott
ys there's a much easier way of proving it than that – by
gonometry or something.'

I walked to my desk and carefully balanced my chalk on the
lge. 'Is Major Faggott teaching you geometry,' I asked,
iving to keep my voice under control, 'or am I?'

'Neither,' said Mason under his breath – but not quietly
ough to save the whole set from being kept in for an hour
is afternoon.

I attribute the indiscipline with which I had to deal this
orning entirely to the influence of Faggott. When one of the
aff, however temporary, swaggers about the place setting
les at naught, ridiculing the school customs, smoking in the
rridors and (as I actually heard at lunch today) openly
lmitting his intention of running up to Town to see one of
e most *risqué* musical-comedies of the day, how can one
xpect the boys to remain uncontaminated? The last straw, to
e personally, came this afternoon when in the hearing of
veral quite junior boys, including one new boy, he loudly
ddressed me as 'The Great Wen' – a punning allusion, pre-
umably, to the first syllable of my name. If it were not for an
istinctive dislike of anything that savours of sneaking I should
ong ago have gone to the Headmaster. That I shall do only as
last resort. Meanwhile, as Gilbert says, there are other
ays. . . .

HURSDAY, 9 MARCH

oys are curious creatures. This morning, apropos of some
oint that arose in connexion with percentages, Williamson
sked whether it was true that schoolmasters were to be exempt
rom National Service, and I said I believed it was and
xplained that even in wartime education had to go on. Several
oys said it was a swizz (meaning swizzle). Hopgood II then
dvanced the extraordinary theory that in an emergency
verybody who had a moustache would be compelled to shave
 off. If Mason or Atkins had made such a statement I should

have come down on them pretty sharply, as I wear a sm
moustache myself and have had reason in the past to susp
both these boys of impertinence (though, to be fair, not ac
ally on that subject), but Hopgood II is a quiet studious bo
who, as I wrote in his Report last term, is keen on his work a
should do well. So I asked him, with a smile, what would
the purpose of such an extreme measure, to which he repli
that he thought it had something to do with mustard gas a
that people with moustaches would be more difficult to deco
taminate than those without. This made Mason and some
the others laugh so immoderately that I had to call the set
order.

'That will do,' I said sharply. 'Stranger things than that m
happen in war.'

Etheridge suddenly shouted out 'Beards!' and went ve
red when I asked him to explain himself. He apologized ar
said he had just realized that Hopgood must mean beards, n
moustaches, because you couldn't get a gas-mask on with
beard because it had to be rolled up inside and then it choke
you, or anyway you couldn't see clearly through the eyepiece

'That is as it may be, Etheridge,' I began, 'but we are n
here to discuss whether or not beards can be worn with ga
masks – .'

'Couldn't they cut a slit in the chin part to let the beard out
interrupted Mason rather rudely.

'Say "Sir" if you are speaking to me, Mason,' I reminde
him, but it turned out that he was speaking to Etheridge.

I hoped that this not very edifying discussion was now at a
end, but Williamson, despite a warning frown from me, starte
an argument with Mason about the effects of mustard gas o
beards, objecting that if a beard was left hanging outside th
mask it would be destroyed. Mason said he didn't believe it an
anyway it wouldn't matter much if it was, and Hillman the
chipped in with the remark that it was a pity old Mr Poole (ou
dear old French master, who retired a year ago) wasn't sti
here; they could have put some mustard on his beard an
watched the result.

'He put a good deal on it himself in his time,' Mason said, 'and nothing happened.'

'It grew longer, if anything,' said Atkins.

One of the things every schoolmaster has to learn sooner or later is never to permit, still less to encourage, criticism of his colleagues. Nothing is more fatal to discipline than to appear even for a moment to countenance any lack of respect for another master, whatever one's personal opinions may be (it went against the grain, for instance, to punish Otterway the other day for a remark he made about Major Faggott, but I had to do it); and I certainly did not propose to allow a slighting reference to such a faithful old friend and loyal servant of the school as Mr Poole, just because he was no longer with us. I told them pretty straight that it was cowardly to attack people behind their backs, and I was not going to have it; they would never have dared to suggest putting mustard on Mr Poole's beard if he had been still at Burgrove.

I had forgotten, as a matter of fact, until Mason reminded me of it, that they did actually put salt in the old man's hair one day towards the end of his time here, when he was losing something of his vigour and grip. How it was done remains a mystery. According to one story the salt was sprinkled in his hat; according to another they somehow persuaded poor Poole that it was good for his scalp and put it on with his consent. Yet a third account says that it was not ordinary salt but effervescent, and that the point of the joke (if such it could be called) came when he smoothed down his hair, as was his invariable custom, with a damp brush. But whatever the truth of the matter, it was a cruel prank and nothing, as I told Mason, to laugh about.

'However,' I went on, 'as you all seem so interested in the subject of gas-masks, let me see what you can make of this: In a town of four thousand five hundred inhabitants two hundred and forty of the men were bearded. . . .'

'In Greece,' remarked Sapoulos, 'that would give surprise.'

'How many of the women?' asked Atkins.

I mention these stupid interjections only to observe that a

schoolmaster's success or failure in dealing with young boys depends upon the extent to which he allows himself to be disconcerted or thrown out of his stride by over-eager or ill-timed interruptions. Experience has taught me that to ignore them is often quite sufficient rebuke to the boys concerned. Spoken reproof, except in cases of glaring impertinence or insubordination, is unnecessary and may lead to endless controversy. The golden rule is; Never allow oneself to be side-tracked.

'– what percentage of the population,' I proceeded smoothly, 'would find an ordinary gas-mask difficult or impossible to adjust?'

One or two boys, as usual, wanted the question repeated, but in two or three minutes they were all hard at work. Nothing arouses their keenness so much as a really practical problem to solve, and of course there was the added incentive of ten marks for the first boy to show up the correct answer, nine for the second, and so on. I had hardly had time to jot down the figures myself before Etheridge arrived at my desk to claim the highest mark, followed in quick succession by Hillman, Trench and Williamson. Then Anderson and Atkins had a race, though they know perfectly well that I will not have running or scrapping in the classroom, and ended by knocking over my ink-pot. I whipped open the desk, through the hinge of which the ink was already beginning to pour, and to my dismay found that I had only a small scrap of blotting-paper. The boys helped with what they had, but it was quite insufficient to deal with the situation. There was nothing for it but to send Etheridge off with a note to Major Faggott, who has taken over Rawlinson's duties in charge of the stationery commissariat – loth though I was to ask any favour of the man. I took care to explain the urgency of the case, and so could hardly believe my eyes when Etheridge returned without any blotting-paper but with a brief *unsealed* note from Faggott saying 'Soak it up yourself'.

I put the note in my pocket without a word and went straight along to Faggott's classroom. I found him with his feet up on the desk, reading to the boys, I was quick to notice, from Green's *History of the English People*, though I know

or a fact that Rawlinson uses Oman. 'Hallo!' he said, not
roubling to alter his position. 'Anything wrong?'

I was boiling with rage but controlled myself in front of the
orm and simply said that I was sorry to disturb him in any
vay (with a meaning glance at his feet) but I must have blot-
ing-paper at once, as there had been an accident.

'Well,' he said, 'the cupboard's open.'

I turned on my heel and left the room. It was quite obvious
hat it never entered his head to come along with me and hand
ut the blotting-paper himself in the proper manner. Not that
minded fetching it myself, in a way, but that the stationery
upboard should be left like that, *unlocked* on a *Thursday*. . . .

I shall not, of course, allow the matter to rest there.

SUNDAY, 12 MARCH

*The following entries appear to have been made at different
imes on the same day: the first, I should say, just before
upper, the second, which is not always easy to read and in
places, to tell the truth, is downright illegible, later on in the
evening.*]

Faggott's last day. He goes, I believe, early tomorrow morning, and I for one shall not be sorry to see the last of him. One
learns as a schoolmaster to rub along with all sorts and conditions of men – 'Look for the good qualities not the bad in your
colleagues' is a useful motto, generally speaking, for Common
Room life – but really, for anyone who cares for the good name
of the school and who feels, well, without any snobbishness,
that the teaching of young boys is a job better left to gentlemen
(in the best sense of the word, of course), I must say that the last
fortnight or so has been something of a trial. However, least
said, perhaps, soonest mended.

In view of all that has happened I was thunderstruck, to say
the least, when Gilbert told me quite casually this afternoon
that Faggott proposed to hold a farewell party in his room
after supper and hoped I would come along. I thought it
typical of the man's monstrous cheek and said so; wild horses,
I told him would not drag me to any party of Faggott's – even

one which was to celebrate his departure. But Gilbert was mo*
persuasive. After all, he said, the man was going and what wa
the use of bearing a grudge? 'Besides,' he added with a wink
'I happen to know that Faggott is going to see the Squid a
half-past ten tonight.'

'Steady!' I said, glancing anxiously round to see if any c
the boys had heard the disrespectful term. 'They'll be out o
the boot-room in a moment. Anyway, what has Faggott's inter
view with the Headmaster got to do with it?'

'Well,' Gilbert said, 'it has occurred to me that if it's prett
obvious, even to the Reverend Saunders, that Faggott has been
celebrating when he goes to see him, there won't be much ris
of Faggott getting asked here again, if you see what I mean
You don't want him back, do you? Very well, then, that's why
I want you to come. The more there are of us, the merrier h
will be. See the point?'

I confess I did not altogether care for Gilbert's suggestion
even if, as I half suspect, he only meant it in fun, but remem
bering what he had said about not bearing a grudge and so
on, I consented to look in at Faggott's party for a few moments
It is to be at eight o'clock, apparently. Supper is at seven here
on Sundays.

The Headmaster was bitterly resentful of his attitude. Bitterly.
Look at my trousers. My coat and trousers are not what they
were not what they were. What will Matron say when she sees
my trousers and my coat and trousers? Trousers trousers
trousers trousers trowsers? trews rather. *Bracæ*=trews. What
will Matron say? It is no business of hers. None at all. My
trousers are my own pigeon as I told the Headmaster. I regret
his attitude and I told him. Bitterly.

'WHO PUT THAT PIGEON IN MY TROUSERS?'

Never mind the pigeon now, Wentworth, Esq., B.A. Let me
tell the story in my own way. I went to Faggott's room and
Collingridge and Gilbert and Rawlinson has been ill but there
he was. I am Senior Mathmatics master at Burgrove Preparatory School and I went to Faggott's room. Mathmatics
mathematics. Who put the 'e' in mathematics? Stand up the

boy who put the 'e' in mathematics. I have been at Burgrove for seven years and in all my seven years at Burgrove I have never had such a thing happen. Never. The long and short of it is that Gilbert was in Faggott's room and Faggott was there and we all sang. I had a whisky and Faggott sang. I like Faggott and I had a whisky because he is going away. Mind you, there was a time when things were different. Not the same. But now they are the same all right and I like Faggott. Then he sang again and I had another whisky because I like him. While he was singing I told him so. 'I bear no grudge,' I said, and he was pleased. Then we all had whiskies and I sang. We all sang. They all sang. He was about to have sung. *Cano – canare*. CANARY! See the point, Mason? *cano – canary – cantuar*. The Archbishop of Canterbury sang!

I fell in a puddle and tore my trousers. The fact of the matter is that Faggott was drunk. Faggott was drunk when he went to see the Headmaster and I ran after him to stop him. Good old Faggott. They tried to prevent me but I ran after him and fell into a puddle in the dark and tore my trousers. So I did not catch him until he reached the Headmaster's door. I seized his coat-tails as he was going in and he lost his balance and fell, but he did not tear his trousers. I am certain of that. He simply fell backwards on the floor and lay there while I spoke to the Headmaster. I went straight up to the Headmaster and took him by the lapels. 'I bear no grudge, Headmaster,' I said. He did not seem to understand, so I showed him the state of my trousers and asked him what in the world he thought Matron would have to say about them. Then Faggott pushed me aside. I was upset and began to sing 'Asleep in the Deep'. Anybody would. But after a while the Headmaster came up and told me to go back to my room at once and get to bed. He said that unless such a thing ever happened again he would say no more about it. He will regret that. I pointed out that I was Senior Mathematics master at Burgrove Preparatory School, which was true. But his attitude was contumacious. I told him his attitude was contumelious. Then I said good night, as I had done all I could for Faggott for the time being.

When I had got out of the room I remembered something and went back.

'It's about my trousers, Headmaster,' I said. That is what I resent so bitterly. I have done my best and the Headmaster's attitude is contumelious, as I told him. Afterwards . . .

Summer Term 1939
Prelude to Disaster

othing, I suppose, can now stop the story getting about. I
ame the Headmaster for this. Had he listened quietly to my
xplanation, as I think I had a right to expect, instead of wil-
lly misinterpreting the situation in which he chanced to find
e, the whole ridiculous affair would have been cleared up,
y coat would have been on and the fishing-rod back in its
lace long before Wilson and Tremayne peeped into the boot-
oom. As it is, goodness knows what wild rumours the boys
ill spread about the incident. Already some young ass has
halked 'LOBSTER POTS. KEEP OFF' on the top of the boot-
ckers; the next thing I suppose will be ground-bait on the
oor of my form-room and similar follies. Well, I shall know
ow to deal with that kind of humour.

Looking back I cannot see that I acted unwisely at any
oint, given the unusual circumstances in which I found
nyself. If the Headmaster cannot understand why I should
vant my umbrella at eleven o'clock at night, it shows a want
f sensibility on his part, not any lack of sense on mine. The
act is that I did *not* want my umbrella, in one way, for it was
a fine starlight night and I had nowhere to go – unless it had
ccured to me to go for a walk at that improbable hour of
night – which I should never have done had it been raining,
naturally. I simply wanted to know where my umbrella was.

I had expected it to be down at the cottage, actually, but
noticing quite by chance that it was not in its usual corner in
the hall I had a hunt in my bedroom and still failed to find it.
I became rather worried and as it was a fine night decided to

set my mind at rest by strolling up to the school and having
look in the Common Room cupboard – not the cupboard
the Common Room, where we keep our gowns, but the tall or
just outside where cricket bats and so on are kept in the wint
and footballs in the summer. What the Headmaster cann
seem to see is that it was only *because* it was a fine night that
was looking for it at all. It would have been madness to wa
up to School through a downpour simply to see whether m
umbrella was there or not.

At any rate I went straight to the cupboard, not troublir
to switch on the lights for I had my torch with me, and ha
just ascertained that my umbrella was *not* there when
stepped back on to a cricket ball, and, in saving myself from
tumble, had the ill-fortune to smash my torch against the wal
So I had to grope my way out of the cupboard in the dark an
in doing so dislodged Gilbert's fishing-rod which fell with
clatter to the floor. Rather carelessly, in my opinion, though
am no fisherman, he keeps it set up ready for an occasiona
afternoon with the grayling, instead of taking it to pieces whe
he has finished with it. Luckily I found the rod after a littl
trouble, by sweeping about with my hands, and stood it u
again in its corner. Then I turned to go out, but to my astonish
ment as I moved the rod fell down again. When the same thin
happened a third time I decided to leave the rod where it wa
until I had put the lights on and could see what the troubl
was. I had not yet realized of course what had happened. Bu
the moment I took a step into the corridor I felt somethin
pluck sharply at my clothing at the back and a kind of gratin
scream came out of the depths of the cupboard. I am not easil
rattled – I should hardly be a schoolmaster if I were – but
confess that for a moment my blood ran cold. Then I pulle
myself together, put my hand behind my back and grasped th
gut that was holding me fast to Gilbert's rod and reel.

By ill-chance the hook had caught me firmly between th
shoulder blades, out of reach, and though I might have broke
the gut I did not care, except as a last resort, deliberately to
damage a colleague's property. I was now in something of a
dilemma. Had it been merely a question of getting to the light-

vitch in the corridor the problem would have been relatively mple; but it was not, for all downstairs lights in the school uildings are controlled by a master-switch behind the boot-oom door, and this the Headmaster himself switches off every ening at half-past ten. It was out of the question to attempt make my way to the boot-room with the reel screaming ehind me at every step. I should have woken every boy in the ouse. I therefore decided, as I think rightly, to take the rod ith me to the boot-room (carrying it of course in my hand). o avoid further noise I re-entered the cupboard backwards n my hands and knees, or rather on my knees and right hand, r with my left I kept contact with the line. In this way I had o difficulty in finding the tip of the rod. Then working my ngers down until I grasped the butt I rose to my feet and left ue cupboard for the last time.

It was no easy journey to the boot-room. If I raised the oint of the rod too high the result was a sharp tug at my aoulders and a warning scream from the reel, while to lower it oo much was to run the risk of entanglement in the slack. It as, I suppose, fear of this latter disaster that made me raise ie point too sharply after manoeuvring it carefully through ie boot-room door. Unknown to me, the line at the very tip of ie rod looped itself round the hasp of the fan-light over the oor, and inevitably at my next step forward the coat rose on ay back, the rod quivered in my hands and a yard of line was ripped with great violence from the reel.

There was now only one thing to be done. I leaned the rod gainst the door-jamb, removed my coat and lowered it with reat care to the floor, at the same time keeping one hand on he rod in case it should be pulled over by the movement of the oat. I was now of course free and very soon had the master-witch down and the boot-room light working. Then I picked p the rod and, stepping on to the boot-lockers, lifted the line lear of the fan-light hasp.

That the Head should appear at this moment was only in eeping, I suppose, with the miserable ill-fortune I had met ith all through.

'Ah, Wentworth,' he said. 'I thought I heard a noise.' Then his eyebrows went up.

'Do you often come here to fish?' he asked.

'I was worried about my umbrella, sir,' I began, realizing at once that until he knew what had happened my behaviour must seem very odd, 'and as it is a fine night – ' but he cut my explanation short.

'I see,' he said. 'And you thought a little fishing would take your mind off your worries? You have foul-hooked your coat, I notice.'

'This rod was in the Common Room cupboard, Head-master,' I explained, stepping down off the lockers, 'and as you can see, the hook caught my coat while I was looking for my umbrella. It is Gilbert's rod,' I added.

The Headmaster still looked dubious. 'It's a long cast from the cupboard to the boot-room, Wentworth,' he objected.

'My coat was in the cupboard, sir,' I said with some im-patience. 'If you would allow me to explain the whole thing –

'No, no,' he said. 'No. I don't wish to pry into my masters affairs. I have no objection whatever to your fishing in the cupboard, provided the boys are not disturbed. But I do think it ought to stop there. I *cannot* understand how you come to be in your shirt-sleeves in the boot-room, considering – What do *you* want?'

He had turned sharply, and to my dismay I caught a glimpse over his shoulder of Wilson and Tremayne in their dressing-gowns.

'I – we're sorry, sir,' said Tremayne, looking at my fishing-rod with his eyes popping out of his head. 'I didn't know – we thought we heard a queer noise – '

'Get off to bed, both of you, at once,' ordered the Head-master, and when they had run off, he turned back to me and made the most inexplicable remark.

'You and your umbrella, Wentworth,' he said. 'You'll be the death of me yet.'

What is particularly puzzling is that this is the first occasion, so far as I know, on which I have even mentioned my umbrella to the Headmaster.

train,' I read out to my IIIA boys, 'leaves Edinburgh for
asgow at half-past three, arriving at its destination – Well,
at *is* it, Etheridge?'

I understood him to say that the half-past three from Edin-
rgh now left at quarter to four, or some such rubbish.

'Are you trying to be funny?' I demanded sternly.

I think he was genuinely surprised by my attitude, for he
shed up to the roots of his hair and answered quite seriously,
ood lord, no, sir. It's the summer time-tables, sir. They've
t the three-thirty Glasgow train back fifteen minutes so as to
nnect with the one-fifty two – '

'Etheridge lives in Edinburgh, sir,' explained Mason in his
erfering way.

'He's nuts on *Bradshaw*, too,' added Atkins. 'I'll bet he's
ht, sir.'

I thanked them all for their assistance, and pointed out that
the purposes of the problem I was about to ask them to be
od enough to undertake, it was really immaterial whether
heridge lived in Edinburgh or Clacton-on-Sea. 'Nor,' I
ded to clinch the matter, 'do I care a brass farthing if
adshaw says the half-past three train starts at breakfast-time.
n not "nuts on *Bradshaw*", Atkins.'

'I only thought we might as well have it right, sir,' said
heridge.

'Can't you see, you little nanny-goat,' I cried in exaspera-
n, 'that we are not concerned with what actually happens
w! I am giving out a sum, not arranging a Sunday outing
the Clyde.'

'Oh, Sunday?' Etheridge said. 'She doesn't run on Sundays.'

'I see,' I said ironically; 'she doesn't run on Sundays. Well,
everybody has made a note of that important fact, perhaps
: can get on with our work. Doesn't run on Sundays, indeed!
e shall have Mason asking for a non-smoker, next.'

When the laughter raised by this sally had died down I gave
em the remaining details of the problem, namely that the
ree-thirty arrives in Glasgow at five o'clock whereas a train

leaving Glasgow at the same time reaches Edinburgh in exac
two hours. The distance between the two places is given as si
miles (Etheridge opened his silly mouth at this, but I quieter
him with a frown), and the problem is of course to discover
what distance from Edinburgh the two trains meet.

I had hardly finished speaking before Williamson, rather
obtuse boy, began to protest that they couldn't do that with
knowing the speed of the trains.

'*Think*, boy,' I implored him. 'How far apart are the t
stations? Sixty miles? Right, and how long does the tr
from Glasgow to Edinburgh take? Two hours, doesn't it? V
well, then. Now, can you tell me the speed in miles per hou
'No, sir.'

'No, Williamson?'

'No, sir. At least – no, sir, not unless I know how often
train stops.'

'There are no stops whatever, Williamson,' I told h
wearily. 'You can take it that the train is an express.'

'Sixty miles in two hours!' cried Mason. 'Golly, what
flier!'

'Get on, Mason,' I said sharply. 'All right now, Willia
son?'

'I think so, thank you, sir. Except what about the other tra
the one going from Edinburgh, the three-thirty, sir?'

'They're both three-thirties, fool,' said somebody, k
though I whipped round like a flash I wasn't quick enough
catch him.

'What about it?' I asked, returning to Williamson.

'I mean, does it stop?'

'It stops at Airdrie,' put in Etheridge before I could spe:
'If you mean the three-forty-five, that is.'

'In here at two-thirty sharp, Etheridge,' I ordered, losi
patience. 'And you too, Mason, if you can't stop that idio
grinning. We are wasting far too much time. Both trains
you'd better listen to this all of you, because I'm not going
answer any more questions – both trains are expresses and r
at a constant speed from start to finish.'

'In that case, sir,' objected Atkins, 'I don't see why one of them gets there first.'

'Tell him, somebody.'

'Because it's got farther to go,' suggested Williamson.

'Oh, jolly good, Batty!' one of them shouted, and not being able to think of a better comment myself I let it pass.

Shortly after this I left the form-room for a moment, ostensibly to fetch a book from the Common Rom, but in reality to stop the boys asking questions and force them to work the difficulties out for themselves. In the corridor I met the Headmaster.

'Hullo, Wentworth,' he greeted me, taking my elbow. 'I've been wanting a word with you. You never told me the real history of that fishing trip of yours the other night. I'm dying to know.'

'As I think I told you in the boot-room at the time, Headmaster,' I began stiffly, 'I was merely looking for my umbrella – '

'*Because* it was a fine night.'

'Exactly. And as – '

'Did you find it?'

'No,' I said. 'Unfortunately not. It was extremely dark in the cupboard as you can imagine – '

'And you took Gilbert's rod by mistake? I see.'

'There was no mistake about it, Headmaster,' I said warmly. 'I may be all kinds of a fool, but I can still distinguish between my umbrella and a nine-foot fishing-rod, I am thankful to say.'

'Then you took the rod to the boot-room on purpose?'

'The point is,' I explained, 'that I could not leave the cupboard without it. So, rather than spend the whole night in the cupboard, I took it with me.'

'Remember, a term or two ago, how you took a maidenhair fern out of my study, Wentworth? I thought at the time it was some sort of uncontrollable impulse that came over you, and I suppose this – this sudden desire to fish comes in the same category, eh?'

But for a twinkle in the Headmaster's eye I should have been seriously annoyed at this reference to a silly misunderstanding that once occurred over a pot-plant of his. Not that the plant was of any particular value to me or anyone else, as it happened.

'If you would let me show you exactly what happened Headmaster?' I suggested.

He turned away and stood with his back to me for a while looking out over the playing fields.

'You mean,' he said at last, turning round with an expression I could not quite fathom, 'you mean – go in the cupboard again?'

I nodded, and he at once agreed to come and watch my demonstration after lunch.

'Half-past two, Wentworth,' he said, adding rather inconsequently, 'I'll send the School out for a walk.'

Thinking it over, I am not sure that I have been wise; I doubt whether any good will come of it. For one thing, of course, I have had to let Mason and Etheridge off detention.

WENTWORTH RE-ENTERS THE CUPBOARD

[*I am indebted to Mr Charles Gilbert for the following account of what took place that afternoon. Mr Wentworth himself is silent on the point.*]

Anybody who has known Wentworth for more than a couple of minutes is aware that however much of a clown he makes of himself, whatever fantastic predicament he gets into he will not leave the thing alone. He will not rest until he has proved to his own satisfaction, and attempted to convince everybody else, that the whole affair was perfectly natural really. If he was found hanging by his braces from the dome of St Paul's (and nobody here would be the least surprised if he were) he would put it down to negligence on the part of the Dean, coupled with a certain amount of sheer bad luck on his own part. 'In attempting,' he would say, 'to make my way out of the Whispering Gallery I had the misfortune to catch my foot. . . .'

Undoubtedly it was this feeling that led Wentworth to give a demonstration to the Headmaster of the way in which he got snared in my fishing-line, and to show how inevitably this mis-

nce compelled him to climb on to the lockers in the boot-
m, with my rod in his hand, and his coat, firmly hooked,
ing out its life on the floor.

awlinson and I knew nothing about this demonstration,
a matter of fact, until just before it was due to begin. We
pened to be talking to Wentworth, who was hanging about
side the cupboard by the Common Room door, when the
dmaster came along.

Ah, Wentworth,' he said. 'I see you've got quite a gathering
it.'

Gilbert and Rawlinson are just off for a walk, sir,' Went-
th explained.

No hurry,' I said, 'if we can be of any use.'

Well, Gilbert,' old Saunders said, 'you ought to be present,
t was your rod,' and he explained, not without a certain
iculty in controlling his voice, what Wentworth was going
o.

o we saw the whole thing.

Wentworth began with a long rigmarole, which I cannot
mpt to follow in detail, about his umbrella. The upshot of
emed to be that as he didn't want it the sensible thing to do
to come up in the dark and look for it in the games cup-
rd. Asked by Rawlinson whether he kept his umbrella in
games cupboard, he said, 'Of course not,' which settled
t point. Then he went into the cupboard, still talking.

You can imagine, Headmaster, that when I lost the use of
torch it was pitch dark in here. It is pretty dark in here
v, even by day, as you can see.'

Ve all crowded into the cupboard after him, to see just how
k it was, and Rawlinson, with a stroke of genius, shut the
r 'in order to reproduce as closely as possible the actual
ditions'. It was now very dark indeed, and we were jammed
tightly together that I could distinctly feel old Saunders
king all over with suppressed laughter. I was, as a matter
act, shaking myself.

What did you do then, Wentworth?'

My first thought naturally, Headmaster, was to get some
t, and I therefore made my way – I beg your pardon, sir.'

'It's all right,' said Rawlinson, 'that was *my* foot.'

'If we could have a little light – Ah! What's this?' Th͘ was a slight clatter and almost simultaneously I was bu͘ violently by Wentworth, who appeared to be sweeping ͘ floor with his hands.

'Let go my leg,' cried the Headmaster suddenly, and ͘ mediately burst into uncontrollable laughter. Only Wentwo͘ was still able to speak and he, in rather a querulous voice, ͘ asking why somebody didn't open the door.

Somebody did, from the outside, and we heard the in͘ nant voice of Miss Coombes (our music lady) demand͘ 'What are you boys doing in there? Come out at once!'

I doubt if a more sheepish lot ever trailed out of a cupbo͘ than the Headmaster and staff of Burgrove Preparat͘ School.

'Why, Mr Saunders!' she cried. 'I – I'm sorry to – to h͘ interrupted you, but I thought perhaps – '

It was an awkward little scene. Only Wentworth, who ͘ been through too much, I suppose, to be concerned abou͘ straightforward situation like this, looked altogether at ease.

'I've got it, you see, Miss Coombes,' he said, flourishing ͘ umbrella. 'I had an idea it might be in there, all along.'

When Miss Coombes had left us, very red in the face, ͘ Headmaster rounded on Wentworth.

'So that's what you had round my ankle, you old rascal. Y͘ would have had me over, if there had been any room to ͘ down in.'

Wentworth pointed out gravely that there had of cou͘ been more room on the night he had first looked for ͘ umbrella. 'I was by myself, you see,' he explained, and ͘ agreed that this was just as well.

The rest of the demonstration went off almost withou͘ hitch. We got him hooked up, as directed, and off he went w͘ a March Brown firmly anchored in his coat at the back and ͘ rod clasped in his right hand – exactly as on the night, exc͘ that he was not on that occasion carrying his umbrella as w͘

He showed us how, on entering the boot-room in search ͘ the light-switch, he had raised the point of the rod too high a͘ o, 'as ill-luck would have it', got the top of the line looped round the hasp on the fan-light. He had first become aware of this, 'you will understand, Headmaster,' when he felt a jerk and heard more line screaming off the reel; and he demonstrated the jerk and the scream most convincingly. But he failed to notice, and we felt it unnecessary to point out, that on this occasion the reel had overrun, so that a loop of slack line was left hanging between the reel and the first eye on the rod.

I need hardly say that Wentworth put his foot through this loop. It is a fairly easy thing to do, but nobody could have done it more easily than he did.

'Hullo!' he said. 'I'm caught.'

'Did this happen when – on the night?' we asked.

'No. Oh, no,' he said, smiling. 'This is an unrehearsed effect.'

He was standing on one leg now, trying to scrape the line off his right calf with the point of his umbrella. When he began to lose his balance I had a moment's uneasiness, for I feared he might put his right foot down too abruptly, trying to save himself, and thereby snap the point of the rod. But I need not have worried. With the umbrella between his legs he never had a chance, and after spinning right round twice like a top he had to confess himself beaten and went down with all hands into the boot-basket.

'Are you hurt, old chap?' I asked, as soon as I could speak.

'No, no,' he said, struggling to get up. 'I am all right, thank you. But I am worried about my umbrella.'

'You said that the first time,' cried the Headmaster, and rushed off hooting, I regret to say, like a madman.

We could hear him, far off down the corridor, beating his knees with his hands and repeating at intervals with a kind of incredulous awe, 'He's worried about his umbrella! Oh, my aunt, he's *still* worried about his umbrella!'

FRIDAY, 23 JUNE – EVE OF FOUNDATION DAY

I felt tired and depressed when I woke up today. The depression lasted all morning and I found it difficult to concentrate on my work, with the result that in working out a sum concerning the price of eggs my mind wandered to the wall-papering problems which we did last week. This led me to attempt to find the perimeter of the eggs in feet and inches, which of course, not knowing the measurement of the eggs, I could not do. I rubbed it all out and began again but was still muddled and got an answer giving the number of eggs (which of course we knew already) instead of their price. Very un-willingly, for I dislike anything that savours of subterfuge, I explained to the boys that I had done this in order to test them and called Mason up to point out where I had gone wrong. He said that he couldn't see anything wrong with it except that it was a mistake to try to paper a room with eggs – at which we all laughed. He asked for a mark, which I allowed, perhaps unjustifiably, but I was in no mood for argument, and I offered to double it if he could work out the sum correctly himself. He said, 'Let x be an egg.'

I told Etheridge to stop tittering and nodded to Mason.

'Well, sir, then twelve eggs equal $12x$.'

'Well?'

'Then 94 eggs equal $12x$ multiplied by 94 over 12, that's to say, sir – er – 94 eggs equal – um – $94x$.'

'I see,' I said. 'So 94 eggs equal $94x$. Go on.'

'So, you see, sir, as 94 eggs cost ten shillings therefore $94x$ equals ten. Then if the price goes up a halfpenny a dozen, the cost of a gross – at least, wait a minute, sir, if 94 eggs equal $94x$ then surely x equals one?'

'One what?'

'One egg, sir.'

I threw up my hands. 'What on earth is the good of that, Mason?' I asked.

The boy looked genuinely surprised. 'That's the value of x, sir. I thought that's what you wanted.'

'Do you mean to say that that is your answer?'

He said it was, and when I told him to sit down, calmly asked for another mark. It is this kind of attitude that makes a schoolmaster's task so unnecessarily difficult and wearing. Boys like Mason make no attempt to get to the root of a problem, they simply let x equal anything that occurs to them, whether

has any bearing on the sum or not, and imagine that by
multiplying and dividing it they will arrive at some sort of
answer and perhaps get a mark for their trouble. Naturally it
particularly annoying to find them using x in a sum of this
kind which does not call for the introduction of an unknown
quantity. I worked the problem out again myself, getting it
right this time – only to find Hillman drawing horses on his
blotting-paper (a silly trick) and Hopgood II asleep. There is
something wrong with Hopgood II, I think, but whenever I
speak to Matron about his drowsiness she merely says that none
of the other masters have complained of his going to sleep in
their forms. As if that had anything to do with it.

After dinner this evening I went to see the Head on some
small point about Common Entrance papers, forgetting that
tomorrow is Foundation Day here and that the Bishop of
Puntsbury, who has kindly consented to preach at the morning
service, would naturally be staying the night. However, the
Headmaster made me welcome, cutting short my attempted
explanations with a genial 'No shop now, Wentworth!' and
invited me to take coffee with them. I accepted and we had a
pleasant chat.

The Bishop seems to be a man with wide interests, not at all
'churchy' or wrapped up in narrow diocesan affairs. He was
talking about the Bren gun when I came in and good-naturedly
included me in the conversation by asking whether I could tell
him the average life of the barrel. I said I had no idea, and
asked him in my turn whether he by any chance knew a Canon
Hanford, who had, I believed, or used to have, associations
with Saintsbury. He said he did not, but he knew, of course,
Lady Slinford, the niece of the Earl of Belsize, who had
recently married one of the Worcestershire Frumps – or some
such name. I replied with a smile that so far as I knew the
Canon was not connected with any noble family, whereupon
he turned to the Headmaster and began to talk to him about
Swedish pom-poms – all Greek to me. Apparently the Bishop
had been dining recently with a member of the Cabinet who
had him in confidence that their manufacture was going ahead
by leaps and bounds. Then the conversation turned to tanks.

Mr Saunders ventured to observe that he supposed the day
the horse in warfare was over, but with this the Bishop co
not altogether agree.

Hearing the horse mentioned and not wishing to be left
of the conversation, I quoted the first apposite line from
Bible which came into my head, 'The glory of his nostril
terrible.'

'Whom do you mean, sir?' asked the Bishop, wheel
round.

I explained that I meant the horse and added 'Ha
among the trumpets' to make the reference clear. Our visi
replied with a grunt and seeing that he was becoming tir
not unnaturally, of this rather military talk, I put a questi
to him about his diocese, which I had always understood to
largely agricultural and therefore at the moment goi
perhaps, through a rather difficult time. But he misundersto
my meaning, replying that the chief trouble was a serie
shortage of ambulance drivers and quoting figures wh
seemed to relate, so far as I could follow them, to the Auxilia
Fire Brigade. This talking at cross-purposes confused me a
I said good night and took my leave without remembering
ask, as I had intended, about the Lessons for tomorrow. P
sumably the Headmaster will read the second, leaving 'Let
now praise famous men' to me, in the ordinary way, but it
just possible he may wish to spare his voice, in view of
Speech, and in that case Rawlinson should, I suppose,
warned. I returned to the study to make sure, but finding t
Bishop on the floor expounding some point in connexion wi
high-angle fire, crept out again without disturbing him.

It is all rather puzzling. But no doubt everything will go
splendidly tomorrow.

SATURDAY, 24 JUNE — FOUNDATION DAY

And what a day it has been! No school, of course, but a gre
deal to arrange and the prizes to see to, and so on. It would
do to have any hitch at the last moment with all the parents
their places and our whole organization *sub judice* so to spe
or whatever the expression is. There *was* a bit of a difficulty,

matter of fact, because the wrong *Decline and Fall* had been ant – nothing to do with the Roman Empire as far as I could e on a hasty inspection, and in places hardly suitable for oung boys. When I pointed this out to the Headmaster immediately after breakfast, he laughed and said it was lucky they adn't sent the right one or we should never have got it all into ae gym (where we have the prize-giving nowadays).

'But what are we to do, Headmaster?' I asked. 'Baylis will e terribly disappointed if there is no prize for him.'

He said he was very busy and had every confidence in my bility to do what seemed best – all very well, but I cannot be xpected to conjure books out of thin air, especially on a day ke this when I have enough to do in all conscience and the rhole place is swarming with parents determined to get hold f one and talk about their boys. However, I managed to find 'hring, whose parents are in India, and arranged that after eceiving his copy of *Ivanhoe* he should hand it at once to one f the senior boys who would unobtrusively return it to the able. It could then be presented again to Baylis when his turn ame and nobody need be any the wiser. Of course I promised hat Thring should have another copy as soon as it could be btained. He asked if he might have *Forty Years Under the 'ea*, or some such book, instead. I had never heard of it and loubted whether it would have the same appeal for a boy as *vanhoe*, so I gave a non-committal reply. I don't see that I ould have made any better arrangement on the spur of the noment.

Just before Chapel I met the Bishop taking a stroll down the Avenue and put some casual question to him about Consistory Courts, merely as a means of opening a conversation. To my stonishment he burst into a torrent of what I should have lescribed, in one not of his cloth, as angry abuse, asking me vhat the dickens I thought I was playing at, whether I magined he was the Archbishop of Canterbury in disguise or vhat, and a lot more incomprehensible questions. 'But surely,' said, 'you are the Bishop of Saintsbury?'

It turns out that he is not a Bishop at all, but a retired Colonel who has taken Orders late in life 'for want,' as he

chose to put it, 'of something better to do.' How Gilbert, wh
definitely told me that the Bishop of Saintsbury was comir
down to preach on Foundation Day, came to make the mistal
I do not pretend to know. Naturally when I called on th
Headmaster last night and discovered a gentleman in cleric:
dress in his study I took it for granted that his guest was th
Bishop. It is true I might have paused to wonder why he w:
not in apron and gaiters, but the fact of the matter is I simpl
failed to notice. After all it is no business of mine what bisho;
wear. I have enough to worry about already without that.

'Why then, Colonel,' I said, after begging his pardon fc
mistaking him for a Bishop (an error which seemed to fill hir
with quite unreasonable resentment), 'I wonder if, in you
professional capacity, you ever came across a Major Faggot
who was on the staff here a short while ago?'

'Faggott?' he said, 'Faggott? No, never heard of him. Nc
one of ours, anyway.'

'Whose?' I asked.

'Ours.'

'Oh!' I said, rather at a loss. 'Not one of ours either, really

This for some reason made the Colonel think I was an ol
Army man myself, and after a few minutes' rather fruitles
conversation we parted. His sermon, which took the form o
an appeal to us all to join the Territorial Army, was rathe
wasted on the boys, who have all made up their minds t
become Air Cadets as soon as they are old enough. Still, he i
of course an Old Boy, and we were all glad he was able t
come.

I thought the Headmaster's speech went better than eve
this year. The parents were obviously pleased at his referenc
to the health of the school, which, apart from influenza anc
the mumps epidemic last term, has been uniformly excellent
and they clapped very heartily at the announcement of specia
Rhythmic Exercise classes in the near future for boys whc
wish to take them. In games, the Headmaster said, the schoo
had not perhaps been quite so successful as in some previou:
years, but the general level of performance throughout the
school had never, he thought, been higher, and that, after all

as of more importance than the possession of a few boys of utstanding ability in the First Elevens. Turning to work he xplained that with an unusually young Sixth Form the onours List was necessarily a short one; they would all be etting their scholarships next year. But he had much pleasure congratulating Thomas on his successful entry into the oyal Naval College, Dartmouth. In conclusion he very kindly entioned the unfailing assistance and loyal support he had ceived from every member of the Staff.

Afterwards Lady Portcullis gave away the prizes. Hillman, was glad to see, got the Tidiest Dormitory Prize in his capaty as Aedile of the Junior Green. Aediles, of course, have not e authority of full Praetors (of which there are six), but are ut in charge of the smaller dormitories such as the Junior reen, Admiral Benbow and Upper Far — which used to be lled Eastman's until the tragedy. There was, after all, a uddle about Baylis's prize, because Thring, apparently misnderstanding my instructions, handed his *Ivanhoe* to Baylis, ho was sitting near him, directly he returned to his seat. Then aylis, when his name was called out by the Headmaster, took e book up with him and gave it back to Lady Portcullis. This aturally confused Lady Portcullis who had just been handed *he Lays of Ancient Rome* (intended as a matter of fact for homas) by the Headmaster and, no doubt in order to cover p a moment's hesitation, she asked the boy, very kindly, what s name was. He said it was Thomas, meaning his Christian ame, of course (he is quite a little chap really — only nine), and e thereupon gave him *The Lays*, at the same time conratulating him in a clear voice on passing into the Navy. aylis got very red, but wisely said nothing. This left *Ivanhoe* or Thomas — I mean Thomas, R., of the Upper IV — as his rize for passing the Dartmouth Entrance. He accepted it ithout comment, though I happen to know that he received copy of the same novel last term for his work in Set I. Still, here was nothing else to be done.

On the whole a most successful Speech and Prize-giving.

he Old Boys beat the School by three wickets this afternoon.

An excellent game, though I confess my attention was rather
distracted at times. Several parents came up to discuss their
sons' progress, and in particular I had a long talk with Mrs
Hillman. She is petite with blue eyes and is rather charming
though a little unorthodox. We talked about ballet for a while,
of which I know nothing, and then she suddenly turned to me
and remarked, 'What a funny old stick your headmaster is!'
I was naturally taken aback, especially as other parents and
their boys were standing quite close to us, and I hurriedly
observed that I hoped she would be at the concert in the
evening. But she refused to take the hint.

'Come now, Mr Wentworth,' she said, laying her small hand
on my arm, 'you can't deny it. Look at him talking to that
woman in the wig over there.'

'Really, Mrs Hillman !' I said in a low voice. 'We are not
alone.'

'That isn't my fault, is it, Mr Wentworth?' she replied.

I was absolutely dumbfounded, and before I could collect
my wits she went on in the most confiding way, 'Is he or is he
not a pompous old thing?'

'Well – ' I began, and we both laughed.

We soon became firm friends and she talked in a most
interesting way about several of the parents, many of whom
she seemed to know personally. I pointed out Clarke's mother,
a very striking figure in red, and she remarked, 'It costs that
woman eight hundred a year to look like that.'

'No one would say that of you, Mrs Hillman,' I said
gallantly.

'Meaning that I'm obviously cheaply turned-out?' she
replied mischievously.

I simply gave her a look and she lowered her eyes.

'Here comes that spiteful old cat with the wig,' she said
presently. 'Now watch. Hullo, Peggy. You know Mr Wentworth, don't you? Mr Wentworth – Lady Cleethorpes.'

'How do you do,' I said.

'We were just talking about you,' said Mrs Hillman. 'Mr
Wentworth was saying you looked a spiteful old cat.'

'I assure you, Lady Cleethorpes!' I cried, reddening to the roots of my hair. 'Mrs Hillman is utterly – '

'Did she tell you I wear a wig?'

'I – that is,' I began, completely at a loss for words, 'I should never have guessed – '

'Well, I don't,' said Lady Cleethorpes, and both women went off into peals of laughter.

I felt extremely uncomfortable. People were looking at us – and no wonder. The cricket field, when a serious game is in progress, is not the place for loud laughter. Besides, the whole position was most embarrassing. There seemed to be no knowing what these extraordinary ladies would say next. I determined to bring the conversation back to a sensible level at once.

'How is your husband, Mrs Hillman?' I asked, giving her a reproachful look.

She became serious at once. 'I have no husband – now, Mr Wentworth,' she said.

I murmured a few conventional words of sympathy, cursing myself silently for a clumsy fool, but she cut me short.

'I divorced him,' she said briskly. 'He was no loss.'

'So go in and win, Mr Wentworth,' added Lady Cleethorpes with another of her penetrating laughs.

I may be old-fashioned but I confess I have no use whatever for this kind of talk. Divorce is not a subject for jesting. No doubt, in the world in which some people live, the so-called *haut monde*, it is considered clever and amusing to make light of serious and intimate subjects of this kind, but here at Burgrove we prefer to take a different attitude. Moreover I do not care to be made the object of remarks in, to say the least, doubtful taste, particularly when these involve the good name of a lady who happens to be present.

I made my excuses rather coldly and turned away, not knowing that one of my sock-suspenders had unluckily come unfastened and was trailing on the ground. I might not have noticed had not Mrs Hillman unwittingly set her foot on the metal clasp or fastener so that I was brought up short after a single stride and all but overbalanced. Mrs Hillman very kindly moved her foot in a quite natural way when she noticed my predicament, as if unaware that anything unusual had happened, but Lady Cleethorpes, who seems to be utterly lacking in tact, broke out into another loud laugh and cried, 'You'll have to marry her now.' This was too much for my temper and I fear I might have spoken very sharply to Lady Cleethorpes had not the Headmaster come up at that moment and joined the group.

'Ah!' he said, rubbing his hands together in a way which I am bound to say I sometimes find rather irritating, 'I hope Mr Wentworth has been entertaining you two ladies.'

'He certainly has,' said Lady Cleethorpes.

I left them as soon as I could and wandered off to the far side of the field, where I did my best to forget my annoyance by concentrating on the game. The Old Boys had got to within twenty-five of our total for the loss of four wickets, mainly through Felpman (a mainstay of the Eleven in the old days, though a poor mathematician. Percentages always used to beat him, I remember), and things looked bad for Burgrove. Then Clarke stopped a hot one at extra cover and I joined in the general shouts of 'Play up, School!' Nothing came of it, however.

'Oh, Mr Wentworth,' said a well-known voice, and I turned to find Mrs Hillman at my side. 'I am so sorry,' she said, 'if Peggy annoyed you.'

'It was nothing,' I said stiffly. 'Lady Cleethorpes has perhaps a rather – unusual sense of humour.'

'You're not angry with me, are you?'

I looked down at her kindly, and found to my intense mortification that I was still holding the lose suspender in my right hand. Mrs Hillman followed the direction of my eyes and then, with a discretion that I admired, turned her head away. I stuffed the offending article into my pocket.

'Tell me, Mrs Hillman,' I said, to cover our mutual embarrassment; 'your friend – Lady Cleethorpes – she has no boy here surely? There is no Cleethorpes on the School List. A nephew perhaps?'

'Oh, didn't you know?' she replied, opening her eyes wide in astonishment. 'That's her son over there – that tall good-looking boy in spectacles. She used to be a Mrs Mason before her second marriage, you know.'

'*Mason*?' I cried.

'Yes. Johnny Mason. You must know him.'

'Ah!' I said. 'Yes. Yes, yes. Mason! I see.'

[*Two weeks later occurred the unfortunate affair of Hopgood II and the algebra book which might have had serious consequences for Wentworth's career but for the general amnesty which a world war brings in its train. Early in 1940 he joined the army. A few scattered extracts from the diary of Second-Lieut. Wentworth, R.A. will be found in the next section of this book.*]

An Assistant Master at War

I fell over that coil of rubber tubing again this morning on my way back after inspecting the cookhouse and went straight off and reported it to the Adjutant. The thing is simply a death-trap where it is at present. He said, 'Get it moved, then. You're Orderly Officer at this R.H.Q., aren't you?'

I pointed out that I should hardly care to move a piece of equipment without his authority, but that if he gave that authority I would have it moved at once.

'All right,' he said, 'go ahead and move it. And for goodness' sake, Wentworth, don't come and bother me about every trivial thing that crops up. I'm busy.'

I thought this unfair. It is very difficult for a new officer to know just what he may or may not do without reference to higher authority. I determined to get things clear in my mind once for all.

'May I take it then, sir,' I asked, 'that in future I have authority to move such things as coils of tubing and so on without applying to you?'

'Yes, yes, yes,' he said.

'What about benches and tables?'

'Do you want to move benches and tables, Wentworth?'

'No,' I said. 'But the occasion might arise.'

'Well, when it does arise, for the Lord's sake move them!'

'On my own initiative?'

'On your own flat feet for all I care,' said the Adjutant, throwing down his pen.

'Very good, sir,' I said, keeping my temper, and saluted, not noticing a tray of papers which had very foolishly been placed on top of a filing-cabinet at my right elbow. It took me some little time to collect all the papers and replace them. I am not a young man and quite unused to scrambling about under desks on all-fours. We left that kind of thing to the boys at Burgrove, I am thankful to say. But war is no respecter of persons; I quite realize that.

It was this little contretemps, I think, that made me forget, until I was outside the door, that one point still remained to be settled, and I had therefore to re-enter in order to ask where I was to put the rubber tubing.

To my mind the Adjutant's reply was absolutely inexcusable. No doubt he is a busy man; we are all busy these days. But if I am prepared to take the trouble to ask him a civil question in order to ensure that I carry out my duties correctly, the least he can do is to give a civil answer. After all, we are all in this war to help one another, are we not? Without co-operation, as I tried to tell him, the whole system falls to the ground. Besides, he was the first to complain over that business of the cinders last week. I remember his very words: 'Next time you are thinking of having a lot of smouldering ashes emptied in the ammunition store, just advise me about it beforehand, will you, Wentworth?' Very well. It was simply because of a natural anxiety to avoid any similar misunderstanding over the rubber tubing that I put my question. Surely I had a right to expect a reasonable reply?

I have half a mind to make a complaint.

THURSDAY, 27 MARCH 1941

Old Poole is back at the school, so I hear in a note from Rawlinson. Dear old chap. He left us in 1937 and has come back, I suppose, to take Collingridge's place now the latter has gone into the Navy. I don't know, I'm sure. Collingridge was our English master and Poole taught only French – and not very much of that, I'm afraid – so I don't see how it is going to work out. Probably they will share out Collingridge's work between Rawlinson and that new man Bishop. But then who is going to take IVB? It is all very muddling.

I have been driven almost to distraction by that confounded rubber tubing. I had it put in the miniature rifle range, which has been used as a dump for all kinds of unwanted bales and boxes ever since the war began; but apparently there is a plan to use the range for shooting, and somebody threw the tubing out again into the middle of the drill hall. There the Adjutant found it and made quite a scene, so I'm told; I wasn't there to defend myself, unfortunately. Why he should jump to the conclusion that *I* had put it there, goodness only knows.

The Quartermaster refuses to have it in his store, and the boiler-house seems to be locked every time I try it, so I have ordered two men to push the infernal thing under one of the huts and cover it with cinders. There seems to be no other way out. Of course I intend this to be only a temporary measure.

FRIDAY, 28 MARCH 1941

The question of the disposal of the rubber tubing is settled. Apparently the cookhouse fatigue men use it to wash down the cookhouse floor and so on, and it ought never to have been moved. No one told me this at the time, of course, or I might have been spared a great deal of worry and bother. So it is now back where it started, as I found out quite by accident this morning. I tripped over it, as a matter of fact, on my way back after inspecting the cookhouse.

Another note from Rawlinson by the afternoon post to say that Poole's trousers caught fire during the first period after 'break' yesterday. I must write for details, as I believe there is more in this than meets the eye. Poole was never quite enough of a disciplinarian, to my mind.

15 JULY 1941

A tallish sergeant came into the office this morning while I was reading a Command Order about hair-slides (A.T.S.) and said he was Scringe.

I did not follow what he meant. 'How do you mean?' I asked. 'Are you unwell?'

He said he was Sergeant Scringe.

'Do you mean your name is Scringe?' I asked him, raising

y eyebrows. It seemed to me a most extraordinary thing, ough I remember a boy called Hasty, now I come to think it, in the Upper Fourth and rather good at Greek. Not that is chap looked as if he would be much use at Greek, I must y – or Latin either for that matter. Still, there it is.

'Yes, sir, Sergeant Scringe,' he said. 'Scringe is my name and n a sergeant, sir – by rank of course.'

'Well, what else would you be a sergeant by?' I said – .oyal proclamation? Or what?' I had an idea the fellow eant to be insolent, and I immediately asked him for his umber and pretended to write it down in Command Orders,)t having any other paper handy. I make a point of asking .C.O.s for their numbers if they show any tendency to be uculent. It brings it home to them, I think.

Collingridge used to do the same thing at Burgrove (which ill stands in its own grounds in spite of the bombs, as Gilbert .id in his last letter. He always had a clever way of putting .ings, though the Head told me once – however, I detest)ssip, and after all it's what a man *is* rather than what he *has* :en that counts. Though both are important, of course.). I)n't mean Collingridge used to ask the boys for their num- :rs, because naturally they hadn't any, except on their lockers a the boot-room and so on; it was a help with the washing nd mending, Matron said. He used to ask them their ages istead: '*How* old are you, Fearnly? Ten? Dear me, I should ave thought eight was nearer the mark.' He always said it orked very well, but I don't know. Boys are curious creatures.

I tried it myself once or twice, but not very successfully. Iason said, I remember, that in another eight years he would e twice as old as his father was fifty years ago, and naturally I ouldn't make any comment in case it might appear to be a eflection on Mr Mason in some way. The *first* Mr Mason that ould be, of course, not that the second Mr Mason's name ould be Mason at all, now I come to think of it. Every master as his own way of dealing with boys, I suppose. Mine, I like) think, is to lead rather than drive.

I was thinking rather nostalgically of the old days and the mell of the hymn-books in chapel and mark-reading and so

on and so forth, when the phone rang and a voice said, 'You
through.'

'Through where?' I asked.

'Hold on a moment,' the operator said. 'I'm just getti
them for you.'

'Getting *who*?' I said. 'I haven't asked for anybody.'

Then a man's voice said, 'You're very faint. Can you he
me?' and somebody else asked me whether I was long distan
Of course I couldn't say without knowing where they we
speaking from, and I was pointing this out when the telepho
made a loud jarring noise and drowned me.

'Wentworth here,' I said.

'Hullo!' said the man's voice.

'Hullo!' I said, 'Wentworth here.'

'Hullo!' said the man.

'Hu*llo*!' I said. 'Wentworth speaking.'

'Hullo! Hullo!' said the man.

'This is Crowsfoot double-two-owe-nine-ah,' I said car
fully.

'Speak up Crowsfoot,' said the operator, 'they're callir
you.'

I was on the verge of losing patience when the phone on th
Adjutant's desk began to ring, so I shouted, 'Hold on
moment,' and hurried across. It is always the way when th
Adjutant goes out.

'Hullo!' I said, snatching up the receiver.

'Wentworth here,' said a voice.

I could hardly believe my ears.

'Hullo!' I said, 'Hullo! Hul-LO! Who is it. What is goin
on here?'

'Hullo!' said the man.

'Look here,' I said. 'Were you speaking to me on the othe
phone just now?'

'The *other* phone? What do you mean?' he said.

'I'm speaking on two phones,' I explained.

'No need to do that,' he said. 'There's a mouthpiece an
receiver all in one piece on these new models. You're only givin
yourself unnecessary trouble.'

'Oh, go and boil yourself!' I cried, tired of all this tom-foolery. Then I slammed the receiver down and went back to my own desk.

The telephone there was still crackling.

'Wentworth here,' I said wearily.

'Can you take a call from Bicester, sir?' asked the operator.

'I can take a call from Honolulu if there isn't a raving lunatic on the other end,' I said bitterly. However, it turned out to be the C.O. and I apologized at once, in case he had misunderstood what I had said to the operator.

'What's that, Wentworth?' he said.

'I said I was sorry I said I could take a call from Honolulu if there wasn't a raving lunatic on the other end, sir,' I said.

'What the devil d'you mean, Wentworth?' he said.

I saw I had made a mistake in bringing the wretched business up at all. But there was nothing for it but to go on with it, now it had started. 'I was speaking on two phones, sir,' I explained, 'and I couldn't make head or tail of either of them. There seemed to be a complete fool on the line – '

'There often is,' said the C.O.

'So, naturally, when the operator asked me if I could take a call from Bicester I said – jokingly, sir – that I could take one from Honolulu, provided – '

'Well, don't say it again,' said the C.O., who seemed to be in one of his testy moods. 'Send a car for me at 16.30.'

As usual in this office there was no pencil or paper for me to take the message down, and I was obliged to strike a match and make a note on the blotting-paper with the burnt end. I must remember to speak to my clerk about this absurd shortage of pencils. There is no excuse for it whatever as far as I can see. We were never short of pencils at Burgrove.

As a matter of fact as soon as I had finished my note I caught sight of a pencil under the filing-cabinet, of all places, and had to go down on my hands and knees to fish it out. Imagine my annoyance when I got to my feet to see a tallish sergeant watching me from the opposite side of the desk.

'Well?' I said, flushing. 'What do *you* want?'

He said he was Scringe.

I simply couldn't follow what the fellow meant.

22 JULY 1941

Today started badly. The C.O. complained about the jam at breakfast again, and said the toast was burnt. I do my best but really I cannot be expected to make marmalade out of thin air. Nor do I see what the fact that they have kidneys twice a week at the R.A.S.C. Mess has to do with it. They must be lucky, I suppose. As I said, there is a war on and we must just do the best we can. The Colonel became so unpleasant that I decided to change the subject and began to talk to Roberts, our Adjutant here, about Part II Orders, which I am very anxious to get clear in my head.

'By the way, Roberts,' said the Colonel suddenly, 'Major Bolt was talking to me yesterday about a Sergeant he's got down there – String, Singe – some name like that. Know anything about him?'

'Never heard of him, sir.'

'Scringe,' I said. 'Sergeant Scringe, sir. He came to see me the other day.'

'When was this, Wentworth?'

'The day you were out – you were over at Bicester, I think, sir.'

'The day the car I ordered failed to turn up, you mean, eh?' said the Colonel grimly.

'My pencil had rolled under the filing-cabinet, sir,' I explained, 'and unfortunately the note I made was not very legible, with the result that instead of 16.30 hours – '

'I know, I know,' said the Colonel in his short-tempered way. 'You had been reading a book about Waterloo so you sent the car to Wellington at 18.15. Never mind that now. What did this fellow Scringe want?'

'He didn't say, sir.'

'Well, did you ask him?'

The fact is I was very busy at the time Sergeant Scringe came in. I was speaking on two telephones, which distracted my attention, and what is more I didn't care very much for

e man's manner. With a little encouragement I believe he
ould have become insolent. So I sent him away with a flea
his ear.

The C.O. is a fine type of soldier. I would follow him any-
here, though as a matter of fact he prefers to be on his own
hen he is inspecting and so on. But if he has a fault it is a lack
patience with people who have had less experience of army
fe and ways than he has. After all, if he were to join the staff
. Burgrove, I dare say he would find himself a bit out of his
epth for a term or two and glad enough to take an occasional
p from an old-stager like myself. The boot would be on the
ther leg there, I fancy. I shall never forget Collingridge's first
rm, when he walked across the piece of lawn in front of the
Teadmaster's study. Of course nobody had told him, so he
as not really to blame in any way. I only mean that that is
ie sort of thing that can easily happen to anyone in those
articular circumstances. It isn't quite the same thing as my
orgetting to ask Sergeant Scringe what he wanted, but the
nalogy is close enough to show what I mean.

The C.O. and Roberts were still talking about this wretched
ergeant when I left them and went across to the office. But I
oon forgot him in the normal routine of the day.

French was the first to ring up.

'Look here,' he said, 'about this A/16 of yours.'

'Yes,' I said. 'Which A/16 is that?'

(An A/16 is a thing we attach or 'subjoin', as we say, to a
etter, so that the other man can tear it off and send it back to
how he has had the letter it was subjoined to. If he doesn't
end it, then of course we know he hasn't had it and can send
im another, or have a Court of Inquiry, as the case may be.)

'Dated the fifth,' French said.

'Yes, yes. But what was it attached to?'

'It wasn't attached to anything.'

'Well, subjoined then.'

'It wasn't subjoined either. It was all by itself.'

I saw at once that there had been some mistake. Naturally
one doesn't send an A/16 entirely on its own, because even if
t were returned it would not prove that anything had arrived

– except the A/16, of course, and even that would have con
back.

'Well,' I began, 'it's a most extraordinary thing' – and the
I had an idea. 'You're not talking about a *message* with
reference number A/16 by any chance, are you, French?'
asked.

He said he was, and that of course explained the whol
thing. We might have wasted the entire morning if I hadn
happened to hit on the only possible explanation. After that
was all more or less plain sailing. French complained that ot
A/16 dated the fifth cancelled our A/9 dated the third an
that this in turn had cancelled our A/178 dated the twenty
fifth. He said he wouldn't have minded that, only our A/17
was in fact a cancellation of our letter number four-three
oblique one-three-seven oblique A of 12th May, and h
wanted to know where he stood.

'It's all perfectly simple, French,' I said. 'This four-three
oblique letter was cancelled on the twenty-fifth, then it wa
uncancelled, and now the uncancelling has been cancelled s
that the letter itself is cancelled again. Is that all right?'

'But then,' he said, 'that means there's nothing left.'

'No,' I said. 'The episode is finished.'

'You mean you don't want any nominations for the Wes
Indies after all?'

'No,' I said. 'No, I don't think so. No. Had you got some
body you wanted to nominate?'

'No,' he said. 'Only I don't see what happens to your four
three oblique two-four-nine oblique A dated 8th June in tha
case.'

'Does it matter?' I asked.

He said no, he supposed it didn't, and after a word or two
about things in general he rang off. French is a good officer
but he tends to fuss rather a lot about non-essentials. After all
if a thing is cancelled it is cancelled and that is all there is to be
said about it. Poor old Poole took to reading through his old
mark-lists in his last term or two, which I always thought
rather an unhealthy sign. It's the same sort of thing in a way.

All the same, it's as well to be certain, so I rang for my clerk and told him to hunt up a letter we had written about vacancies for suitable N.C.O.s in the West Indies.

'It's in the Equipment File,' he said. 'Four-three oblique – '

'In the Equipment File!' I cried. 'What in the name of goodness is it doing in the Equipment File?'

'It's Captain Stevens' system, sir.'

Captain Stevens was Adjutant here before Captain Trevelyan, who was succeeded by the present man, Roberts.

'But Captain Trevelyan abolished all that and started a system of his own,' I objected.

'Yes, sir, but when Captain Roberts came he said that of the two he preferred Captain Stevens' system. He said it only meant looking through fifty-six files instead of a hundred-and-ninety.'

Of course I couldn't permit a lance-bombardier to say anything that appeared to criticize something an officer had done, so I sent Hotfoot (another curious name) about his business and settled down to the work of entering up the secret mail.

A Colonel Ferris came to lunch. He is something to do with National Economy, though I must say he ate a good deal. Still, he wears his trousers very short, which sets a good example, I suppose.

He asked me what we did with our old pen-nibs, and I said we wrote letters with them. It seemed to satisfy him.

12 AUGUST 1942

I am to go to a new regiment tomorrow – the 600th. I should call it 'X' or 'B' Regiment normally, for security reasons, but this unit happens to be known simply as 'X' Regiment (another letter, really, of course, but the meaning is clear, I hope), so I thought it safer to reverse the procedure and call it a number. One has to be particularly careful what one says when moving.

It is unsettling somehow to make a change after all this time, but I suppose a soldier must be prepared to up sticks and be off to the end of the world if need be. It is not that I mind, only one gets used to having the hole in the carpet on the right-hand side of the fire-place in the mess and it is disconcerting for the first day or two in the new mess to find it on the left. I have

got used to the filing system here, too, in a way, and there i
the barber in Leopold Street – quite exceptionally good and
very moderate. Goodness knows what the local man at Salisbury will be like.

The C.O. has been most kind. I am not actually appointed
Adjutant of the new unit, he says, but it will be only a matter
of days, he thinks.

13 AUGUST 1942

Well, here I am, with very mixed feelings I must say, particularly as I am not where I expected to be, but somewhere quite
different. At least I don't think I am expected to be here, unless
I made a foolish mistake in the first place, which does not seem
very likely.

The trouble began at the booking-office, where I put down
my railway warrant saying 'Crowsfoot' to the clerk – forgetting
for the moment that it was Crowsfoot *from* which I was going,
not *to* which. The clerk, with a rather impudent grin, said,
'Return?' and somebody in the queue asked me if my journey
was really necessary. I made no reply, but merely stood quietly
waiting for my ticket to be made out. It was all the more
annoying to find that the ticket, when at last I got it, was made
out to the wrong destination.

'Look here,' I said. 'I want to go to Salisbury. You've given
me a ticket to Bury St Edmunds.'

'It says Bury St Edmunds here,' he said, showing me the
warrant, and to my amazement I found that it did.

'There has been some mistake,' I began.

'Your parents', not mine,' said the clerk – a remark of which
I could make neither head nor tail. Surely he did not suppose
that my warrant had been made out by my father, even had
he been still alive, which, as a matter of fact, he is not? Of
course the clerk could not know that, but still! One does not
have warrants made out by one's parents, dead *or* alive.

Unfortunately the train came in while I was wondering
what to do, leaving me no time to ring up my old headquarters
and make certain where I was supposed to go. I still think the
C.O. said Salisbury, but on the other hand there it was in black

d white on the warrant, 'Bury St Edmunds', so rather than
k turning up late at my new unit, which creates a bad
pression, I decided to jump in.

I suppose the difficulty over my ticket had muddled me, for
was not until the train had pulled out that I remembered I
d forgotten to make arrangements about my luggage. I
ppose it will go to Salisbury as it was labelled there, unless it
ys at Crowsfoot. In any case it is extremely awkward to be
this place in borrowed pyjamas, quite apart from shaving
d so on. One feels such a fool.

There were two young subalterns in my carriage who were
ost helpful after I had explained my troubles to them. I was
ubtful at first of the wisdom of telling them where I was
ing until one of them said he was a spy and the other offered
take off his vest and show me the marks of the parachute-
rness on his back, at which we all laughed.

'What would that prove?' I asked. 'Germans use parachutes
well, you know.'

'But haven't you seen the film?' said one of them, staring.

'What film?' I asked.

'*Next of Kin*.'

'No,' I said. 'But I've heard of it, of course.'

'Good for you. Only I thought you must have seen it when
u laughed.'

'Seen it when I laughed?' I said. 'Oh, I see. You mean you
ought I must have laughed when I saw it. But then I haven't
en it, as I told you.'

'No, no. What I mean is I thought you wouldn't have
ughed if you hadn't seen it — '

'Naturally not,' I said. 'One doesn't laugh at what one
oesn't see, does one?' He seemed a particularly incoherent
oung man, even as young men go today, and I turned to the
ther officer and asked him if he could tell me whether the
ooth were at Bury St Edmunds.

He said he thought not, but believed the 500th were at a
lace called Parkinghurst or used to be, if that was any help.
n any case, he said, the train didn't go to Bury St Edmunds
r anywhere near it. This final blow quite disheartened me and

in the end I decided to make the best of a bad business and g
out at Parkinghurst. Rather a dull sergeant at the drill h;
seemed to think I had come to pay the men, but in the end
made myself understood and he agreed to take me to see t
Major.

To my amazement and, I am bound to say, distress, I four
myself face to face with a man who was once, for a short tim
a colleague of mine at Burgrove. In the ordinary way, natu
ally, I am delighted to meet old members of the staff, b
Major Faggott – well really, sometimes I pretty nearly lo
patience with his *laissez faire* attitude and his almost *roisterir*
way of going on. Not a good scholar either. However, there
was.

'Well, well, well,' he said. 'Ruffle my periwig if it isn't o
Wentworth, the doyen of Burgrove. Have a whisky and te
me what brings you here. I suppose you still drink as heavi
as ever?'

'I am on my way to join the 600th,' I replied, ignoring h
last remark, 'and I thought I would report here – '

'This is the 500th,' he said.

'I know,' I said, 'but unfortunately I got into the wron
train for Bury St Edmunds – '

'Bury St Edmunds!' said Major Faggott (he never scruple
to interrupt in the old days, I remember). 'But the 600th aren'
at Bury St Edmunds. All this is very peculiar, Wentworth.
am inclined to think you are a deserter.'

The fool then warned me that anything I said would b
taken down in triplicate and used in evidence against me, an
asked me what I had done with my luggage.

'I have sent it to Salisbury,' I said shortly.

'An excellent plan. Then when you get posted to a unit i
Newcastle and take the wrong train for Haverfordwest you'
find your luggage waiting for you. The only thing is, what ar
you going to do in the meantime?'

'If you will direct me to a hotel,' I began, rather stiffly –
but Major Faggott would not hear of it, and very generously
offered me a bed and the loan of a pair of pyjamas. They ar
rather more gaudy than my usual choice, as one would expect,

t it would have been churlish to refuse. I am sure he means
ll, but, well, I suppose we have rather different ideas of what
and what is *not* done.

AUGUST 1942

e must wait and see what the morrow will bring forth. Major
ggott says I am to regard myself as attached here pending
sting. 'We can always do with another officer,' he said at
eakfast; 'it makes the messing easier.'

'But look here, sir,' I expostulated. 'I've been posted to the
oth. I really think I ought to be getting along.'

'I'll fix that,' he said. 'I'll speak to Charlie about you,' and
plained in answer to my inquiry that Charlie was A.G.6. I
d not quite like to say that I was unaware who or what
G.6 might be, and was therefore obliged to let the matter
op. I suppose it is all right, but really it all seems a little
egular.

'What are we going to do with him?' asked the Major
ddenly. 'We can't very well make him O.C. Transport,
cause there isn't any. At least, we could, of course, in case
me comes along.'

'Gas Officer,' said a tall thin man who had just come in.
Where's the *Mirror*?'

'By the way, this is Hobson – Wentworth. Hobson is my
nnery expert. You wouldn't think he had a glass eye, would
ou?'

'How do you do?' I said. 'I certainly shouldn't. In fact I
n hardly tell the difference even now.'

'Very tactful,' said Faggott, slapping his leg and laughing
ke a madman. 'You've made a friend for life there, Went-
orth. He says he can hardly tell the difference, Hobson, old
oy. The same glassy look in each of them, eh? What?'

'I'm afraid I fail to see the joke, sir,' I said coldly. The fact
, the Major's laughter seemed to me to be in the worst possible
aste. After all, one doesn't laugh at another man's infirmities.

'The joke is he hasn't got a glass eye,' said Faggott, rolling
bout in his chair in the most unseemly way. 'Which did you
iink it was? The dull-green one, or the one with all those red

streaks in it? Oh, dear, oh, dear, Wentworth, you'll be th
death of me yet. "Hardly tell the difference", wasn't it? I mus
make a note of that.'

'I'm afraid I know very little about gas, Hobson,' I said, t
change the conversation. 'I mean, I should have to have
course of instruction before I could conscientiously take on th
appointment.'

However, Hobson assured me that that wouldn't be neces
sary. 'This is a new unit, you see,' he explained. 'Just forming
So nobody knows anything about anything. You'll just hav
to pick it up as you go along.'

'Like a crossing-sweeper,' added Major Faggott, with hi
usual lack of taste.

Apparently my first duty as Gas Officer is to go up in a
aeroplane. I was rather surprised at this, naturally, for I faile
to see the connexion, but Major Faggott explained that we ha
been ordered to send an observer on an air co-operation exer
cise and I was the obvious person to go. He said he believed, a
a matter of fact, that the message was intended for anothe
unit, but it had come to us so we must just carry out instruc
tions.

'But I have never flown,' I objected.

'It's quite easy,' said Hobson. 'You just get in and sit still and
then you get out again when you get back to the ground —'

'Or sooner, as the case may be,' said Faggott.

'You won't be expected to take the controls,' added Hobson.
'The R.A.F. have undertaken to provide a qualified driver.'

'Pilot,' I corrected, *sotto voce*.

15 AUGUST 1942

It has been a most interesting experience. The exercise was at
night, which I hadn't expected, so that one was unable to see
the ground; but, of course, it was the same for the pilot and
the rest of the crew, so I must not grumble.

The R.A.F. were most kind. They gave me a parachute
before we started and explained how I was to use it. 'You
probably won't have to,' my pilot told me, 'unless there are
hostiles about and we get pranged.'

'Pranged?' I said.

'Yes.'

'I see,' I said, though I confess I did not quite follow what meant.

'In that case, just nip out, count three slowly and pull this ng.'

'Right,' I said briskly. 'Does one come down with much of ump?'

'Oh, no,' he said. 'Unless the parachute fails to open.'

'I see,' I said.

It is not very easy to get into a bomber at night, and untunately, when I had got in, there was no seat for me and I d to squat on my parachute.

'By the way,' said the pilot, when we were all inside, 'you've me as an observer, haven't you?'

'Yes,' I said. 'Yes, yes.'

'What are you going to observe, particularly?'

'Well,' I said, 'nothing particularly. Just general observan.' The fact is nobody had remembered to tell me what I is supposed to be doing.

'Afraid you won't see much tonight,' he said. 'Except the rs.'

'It doesn't matter, thanks,' I said. 'I'm a Gas Officer, really. : least, I hope to be when I have had a little more experience.'

'I see,' said the pilot.

Soon after that he started up the engines and conversation ased. It is rather noisy in a bomber when the engines are ing – 'revving', as they say – and one has to shout to make eself heard.

'How high are we now?' I shouted, when we had been aring along for about five minutes. It is quite impossible to t any idea of height when you are flying in the dark.

'We haven't started yet,' shouted the pilot. 'I'm just warmg her up.'

'Oh,' I said, feeling rather a fool. I suppose in the noise and rkness I had got rather confused.

However, it was much the same when we did start, except at one had to shout rather louder. The machine was very

steady, and after a time I became more used to the noise a
began to get ready to observe. Then, without any warni
there was a sudden bump and the aeroplane dropped lik
lift.

I kept my head, and turned inquiringly to the pilot.

'Pranged?' I shouted. But he shook his head and sa
'Cloud.'

'I see,' I cried, but I don't think he heard me.

Nothing happened for another ten minutes and I began
grow aware that my seat was far from comfortable. By p
ill-chance, in endeavouring to adjust the parachute on wh
I was sitting, I caught hold of the wrong handle and somethi
came right away in my hand. I rose to a crouching posit
and, turning round to see what was amiss, was horrified to
a volume of white material, like dough, pouring out of
wrapping. I did not know what to do and the pilot, not rea
ing my predicament, added to my difficulties by turning
machine abruptly on its side so that I was thrown off
balance and forced to put out a hand to save myself. Instan
there was a sharp report and some kind of flare or firework v
projected from the underside of the aeroplane.

The pilot said something which I did not catch, for I h
my hands too full at the moment to attend to him. It is a skil
task, I am informed, to repack a parachute in the most favou
able conditions, and I do not believe it can be done in
crouching position in an aeroplane in the dark. There is
great deal of material to cope with, for one thing.

My great fear was that the thing would master me a
spread all over the aircraft so that we should all be choked
if not that, that the pilot would no longer be able to see t
controls. It seemed to spring up after me the moment I ro
from a sitting position, and do what I would, folds and loo
of the stuff kept oozing out from under me at the sides a
back.

'Sit tight,' I said to myself, 'and keep your nerve', and
remember thinking what a story this would make to tell to t
boys, if ever I should get back to the old life at Burgrove.
think this helped to steady me.

Suddenly I felt a tap on my shoulder and carefully turning out I found that the navigator was trying to communicate th me.

'What do you say?' I cried. 'I can't hear you.'

'Your shirt's hanging out at the back,' he roared.

I realized then that the parachute had got hitched to my m Browne, which I had put on for the flight, and it was this, course, that had given it a tendency to rise up in the air when noved. I unhitched it and had practically no further trouble, am thankful to say.

'I am afraid you were too busy to observe much,' said the ot when we landed.

'Not at all,' I said. 'It has been a most interesting experience r me.'

'It has for all of us,' he said, which I thought very nice of m. After all, one flight more or less in a bomber, even at ght, is all in the day's work for its gallant crew.

here is, of course, a vast mass of material in the war-time aries from which I might quote. But this is perhaps enough show that my friend Wentworth carried with him into the my those same qualities of solid worth and sound logical ommon sense that served him so well in his peacetime profes- on. Mr Wentworth returned to Burgrove after his demobili- ition in January 1946, and the Memorandum with which is book ends shows that he has lost little or nothing of his old air for the big occasion.]

Memorandum from
A. J. Wentworth, B.A.

TO THE HEADMASTER   6 MARCH 19.

Sir – It is with considerable regret that I inform you that thin
cannot go on as they are at present unless some change is mac
Had it been some small matter such as the school radiato
which have been stone cold for the last three days, I shou
have come to see you in the ordinary way, or the shortage
nibs and blotting-paper about which I have spoken fifty tim
to Rawlinson already, but it is *not*. A schoolmaster has plen
to do without that sort of thing in any case. But either there
discipline in a school or there is not. That is my point. And
there is no discipline I for one will have no part in it. I ha
not given up what might have been the best years of my life
Burgrove, in order to have my boot-laces tied to the legs of n
desk at the end of it and so be prevented from rising to my fe
when parents are shown into my classroom, as I always d
This is not the first time an attempt has been made to make n
look ridiculous in front of other people, nor is it the last, as
am well aware, after seeing Matron sneaking into your stu
this very afternoon with some garbled version no doubt of a
incident outside the School Museum which could never ha
happened if people would stop misrepresenting my slighte
action and making mare's nests at my expense out of nothir
at all.

I have always done my best and put the interests of tl
school first, but if it is to be put about that I made an unpr
voked attack with a cutlass on a boy of eleven years during t]
after-lunch rest-period, I can only say that the sooner I tend
my resignation the better for all concerned. That the bc

:olm, was not even a member of my Mathematical Set
d have been enough, one might have supposed, to scotch
a ridiculous story at the outset. But apparently it is not.
sword was not, as it happens, a cutlass, but a scimitar.
e is no cutlass in the School Museum. But those who are
onsible for spreading unfounded gossip of this kind about
re not likely to allow a trifle of that nature to stand in their
. I should be thankful, perhaps, that I am not accused of
wing assegais, of which a large number were presented to
chool last term by Mr Tallboys and hang on the west wall
resent, pending some other arrangement. He has also
nised an elk's head and some West African wood-carvings.
am determined to put a stop to this kind of thing. I have
uch right to handle the weapons in the Museum as anyone.
e. The Museum is in my charge, as was settled at the
ters' Meeting in January, and Malcolm had no business
e there in the rest-period. Does Matron deny my right to
down the scimitar and dust it? If so, let her deny it to my
and I will very soon make clear to her where her jurisdic-
ends and mine begins. She would be better employed in
ng that the boys are resting on their beds after lunch than
ying to interfere with the way I run the Museum.

have little more to say. I consider that Malcolm's
aviour in dashing out of the Museum crying, 'Spare me!
re me!' the moment he caught sight of me with the sword
ny hand was little short of downright impertinence. The
should be thrashed. That I should run after him to tell him
e quiet was not only a perfectly natural thing to do, it was
duty. And I shall continue to do my duty, with or without
tron's permission, for so long as I remain on the Staff here
Burgrove.

That that time is likely to be short we are both well aware.
resignation is in your hands. Should you wish to accept it,
re is no more to be said, except to thank you for many happy
rs and much kindness and to ask you as a special favour that
e arrangement be made to expedite the return of my
ndry before I depart. I should of course in the ordinary way
roach Matron on this matter, but you will understand, in

the circumstances, that that is quite impossible. I have a
books which may be of use to the boys' library.

Should you desire me to withdraw my resignation I wil
so, provided:

That a full apology is made by Matron in the presenc
the whole Staff.

That Malcolm is thrashed, or otherwise punished at y
discretion.

That other arrangements are made for the managem
of the School Museum, which it is now painful for m
enter.

I will take steps to deal with the comparatively trivial ma
of the boot-laces myself.

(Signed) ARTHUR J. WENTWORTH

[*A copy of the note sent by the Headmaster to Wentworth
answer to the foregoing Memorandum, has come into
hands. It seems to clear the matter up.*]

FROM THE HEADMASTER

Dear A.J. – I don't know what all the fuss is about. Mat
came to see me this afternoon about gym-shoes, not cutlas

I have seen Malcolm and told him not to be a silly little fo

The man I had with me when I entered your classroom t
morning was not a parent, or not, at any rate, in the sense
which we use the term; he had come to see about the brea
down in the central heating system. I cannot allow you
resign on the grounds that you were unable to stand up wh
a plumber came into your room.

So please put your personal feelings on one side – a
remember, Wentworth, that the School must come first.

(Signed) G.S.

P.S. I have just completed arrangements for an old friend
yours, Major Faggott, to join us next term in Rawlinso
place. He will probably be willing to take over the Museu
if you really wish to give it up.

By all means use your own initiative about the boot-laces.

The Papers of
A. J. Wentworth, B.A. (Rct'd)

At Fenport

young fellow called at my cottage this morning to ask
whether I would care to become a Vice-President of the
Fenport Football Club. Monday is the day on which Mrs
Bretton takes my laundry home with her and, of course, I was
expecting nothing of the kind.

'Come in, come in,' I said. 'There's nothing else that I know
of, Mrs Bretton, thank you. I put it all together in the bath-
room.'

My visitor said he was Ernie Craddock from the garage and
happened to be passing. I am old enough to remember the days
when he would just have stood there, twisting his cap about
awkwardly in his hands – not Craddock of course, but a much
older man of the same age – and saying nothing. But times
have changed. 'Wash day, eh?' he said. 'Shan't keep you a
tick, though. The thing being, what about you as a Vice-Pre
of the club?'

I said, when I understood what it was that he was trying to
say, that it was a great honour to be asked and one that I
greatly appreciated. 'What would my duties be exactly?' I
asked, and he told me that I should not have to do anything
actually. 'It's just the subscription, see,' he explained.

'I see,' I said. 'Well, I shall have to think it over – Yes, Mrs
Bretton? What is it now?'

She is an excellent creature in many ways, and cooks my
lunch and so on except on Sundays, when her husband is at
home, but she does not understand that there are times when
ones does *not* wish to be bothered with household matters.

'No, not those,' I said, to be rid of her. 'The thin blue stripe

this week, please. I was never a great footballer, I fear, Mr
Craddock,' I went on, 'so that if there were any question of
taking an active – '

'No refereeing, eh? Is that it?' he cried, breaking out into
loud laughter, in which I confess I did not join. I suppose he
intended a reference to a trivial incident that occurred toward
the end of the cricket season, when I was unexpectedly asked
to umpire a local match. The whole thing has been ridiculously
exaggerated. It is nonsense to say that I deliberately tripped up
one of the Fenport batsmen in the middle of the pitch and then
gave him out. I have umpired hundreds of games at Burgrove
Preparatory School in my time, including one or two First
Eleven fixtures when Rawlinson was away, and such a thing
has never happened before. I had a perfect right to cross over
from one side of the pitch to the other, as soon as I noticed that
a left-hander had arrived at my end – indeed it was my duty
so to do.

'The bowler was entirely to blame, Mr Craddock,' I said
with some warmth, when he had had his laugh out. 'He had
no business to deliver the ball without first ascertaining that I,
as umpire, was in a position to adjudicate if called upon to do
so – as in fact I was.'

'The bowler, eh?' he repeated, breaking out afresh. People
often laugh a great deal, I have noticed, when they realize they
are getting the worst of an argument.

'Certainly,' I said. I had no doubt in my own mind that the
bowler was to blame. The result of his precipitancy was that in
crossing the pitch I inadvertently collided with the batsman
who was running a leg-bye, and to add to the confusion he, in
falling, made an involuntary sweeping movement with his bat
and brought down the batsman from the other end. Mean
while the stumps had been thrown down and, on appeal from
the wicket-keeper, I had no option but to give the decision 'run
out'. Even, as I explained later to the Fenport captain, had I
been in any way to blame, there is no provision in the Laws for
'Obstruction of the striker', whether by an umpire or anyone
else. It was simply one of those instances of bad luck, which

ometimes occur in cricket and must be accepted in a sporting
pirit.

'I thought I should have died,' Craddock said, beating his
hands against his knees in a rather affected way. 'The three of
you lying there, and you on your back with your finger up
calling "Out!". "OUT!" says you. "Out! Who's out?" says
somebody. "Both of 'em?" And then, on top o' the lot – '

I enjoy a good joke as well as any man, but I fail to see the
humour in what was, after all, a straightforward cricketing
dilemma. It is true that, on being asked amid some laughter
which of the two batsmen I had given out, I declined to give
a ruling; but my difficulty was that both of them – indeed, all
three of us – lay at a point roughly equidistant from the two
wickets, and I was unable without reference to *Wisden* to say
how the Law stood. I therefore, rightly I think, referred the
matter to my colleague at the bowler's end, who called very
belatedly, 'No ball!' and ordered the game to proceed – a
highly improper decision, in my opinion. Be that as it may, no
one had a right to criticize my own handling of the incident
who has not himself been faced with a similar situation on the
cricket field – at short notice too, remember.

I was endeavouring to point this out to Craddock, and
growing a little heated at his continued silly laughter when
Mrs Bretton, perhaps fortunately, came down again to say that
she had found my spectacles in 'the upstairs place' as she
prefers to call it.

'I have my reading glasses here, thank you, Mrs Bretton,' I
said, taking them out of my pocket.

'These'll be the others then – for looking out the window
and that,' she replied. 'Though what you'd be wanting with
them in the upstairs – '

'Never mind that now,' I said sharply. 'Just leave them on
the table, please.' I have no wish to hurt her feelings, but I
really do not feel that I can enter into long discussions about
where and why I have left this, that or the other thing. I had
enough of that at Burgrove, towards the end.

Craddock took himself off soon afterwards, remarking that
a guinea was the usual thing and adding that he had had 'a

wonderful time' – a glib phrase, meaningless in the circumstances, which I suppose he has picked up from his betters or
the wireless or somewhere. I saw him to the gate and was just
too late to shout at Sidney Megrim's infernal terrier. He pays
no attention whatever to the by-laws relating to footpaths, and
I shall really have to speak to him about it. To Megrim, that is
to say. It is useless to speak to the dog.

When I had dealt with that, it was time to go down to the
village for tobacco, and with one thing and another my *Telegraph* crossword had to be left till after lunch. Not that it
matters, in a way. I am no stickler for a rigid routine, I am
thankful to say. It is just that one likes to have the afternoon
free for other things.

A letter from Gilbert, who will be following me into retirement
in another five years or so, I suppose, set me thinking about the
old days after tea. Or rather, set me thinking after tea about
the old days. One likes to be accurate – I have my mathematical training to thank for that – without being too fussy,
and as a matter of fact it was after breakfast I happened to be
thinking about. This being Monday the Stationery Cupboard
should have been open between 9 and 9.30 a.m., and I could
not help worrying. Gilbert has had a lot of experience, of
course; he knows about the pink blotting-paper for Common
Room use only, naturally. But experience isn't everything, now
that he has taken over full responsibility. One has to be pretty
firm at times, with a lot of boys clamouring round for pens and
rubbers and so on, to which very often they have no right. For
want of a nail, they say, the battle was lost, and the same thing
applies, up to a point, to nibs and Common Entrance. Of
course, it is none of my business now, and nobody I dare say is
indispensable, difficult though it may be at first for my colleagues to realize it. 'We struggle along as best we can,' Gilbert
very kindly writes, 'without you.'

It is a relief, in a way, to be free of the worries and anxieties
of a senior master at a preparatory school, but life without
responsibility and duties, as I told them all at the Presentation,
is an empty thing. ('As empty as a swimming bath without any

water in it,' I could not resist adding, a reference which they greatly appreciated to the time when, through an absurd misunderstanding, I opened the wastepipe on the morning of the School Diving Competition. A joke against oneself helps to relieve the tension, I have often found, even on a serious occasion; though my heart was heavy enough, naturally, as I stood there with my right hand resting on the mahogany bureau subscribed for by many old Burgrovians, as well as past and present colleagues.) 'I hope,' I said to them, when the laughter had died down, 'that I shall find no less useful work to do at my new home in Hampshire.' This, for some reason, started the younger boys laughing again – through over-excitement, I think.

I certainly intend to take as full a part in the life of the village as my reading and other tasks and interests allow. But these things take time. One cannot become a churchwarden overnight. I should have thought that any fool would understand that. I thought so at least until this evening, when I sauntered down to the post office to get my reply off to Gilbert.

I was standing quietly at the stamp counter, waiting until the sub-postmistress had finished selling a pair of canvas shoes, when quite by chance I happened to overhear a conversation between two men at the far end of the shop, one of whom I recognized by his voice to be Mellish from the chemist's.

'Who's that little old chap went up street just now, then?' the other man asked.

'Struts along?' Mellish asked. 'Shortish, and looks over the top of his specs? Name of Wentworth. Elm Cottage. Didn't you hear?'

The other man said no, and Mellish then gave a very inaccurate and one-sided account of the umpiring incident to which I have already briefly referred. I had half a mind to go across at once and point out the fact (which Mellish had deliberately omitted) that it was the bowler who had been to blame. It would have served Mellish right to be made to look foolish in public. But, to tell the truth, I am sick and tired of the silly business, and besides that I strongly object to eavesdropping in any shape or form. I should have made my way out of the shop, had there been any way of doing so un-observed. As it was, I was forced to remain and listen to the rest of the conversation, distasteful though it was.

'What is 'e, then, when he's not playing the giddy-goat?' the second man asked. (Giddy-goat, indeed! My old friends at Burgrove would have something to say about *that*.) 'What's 'e do?'

'Do?' Mellish said. 'Nothing.'

'How's he manage that, then?'

'Easy,' Mellish said. 'Starts right in at it after breakfast, so I'm told, and keeps on without a break till bedtime. A proper gentleman, old Mother Bretton calls him.'

'I should like a threepenny stamp at once, please, Mrs Enticott,' I said loudly. 'I am in rather a hurry, as I have a great deal to do.'

I propose to leave the matter there. At my age one has learnt to treat idle, ill-informed gossip with the contempt it deserves. All the same, I shall be surprised if Mellish does not take a very different view of my character before the year is out.

A Misunderstanding at
the Greengrocer's

I am not at all sure that time is really saved by this modern habit of abbreviation. The longest way round is often the shortest way home, as my old nurse never tired of telling me. She is dead now, of course, but the principle of the thing remains. 'Just you put one leg in at a time, Master Arthur,' she used to say. 'Then we shan't have you toppling over backwards into all that Plasticine.' She had a fund of wisdom, rest her soul, and the world would be a better place if there were more of her like about today.

Her words came back to me at the greengrocer's this morning. I mean about the shortest way home, naturally – not the other. At my age one doesn't topple over backwards at the greengrocer's or anywhere else; or at least, if one does (and the truth is, whatever Miss Edge might say, that the place was abominably crowded and I for one would rather step a little too close to the carrot rack than inconvenience a lady any day), the reasons are different. What made me think of my old nurse was this silly trick of saying 'three' instead of 'three pence' or 'three-pennyworth'. Surely we are not all in such a rush to get wherever we are going that we have time only for monosyllables? The result in any case is to waste time as often as not, as happened this morning when I said I wanted some brussels sprouts and asked the price.

'Ten,' the man said.

I naturally supposed he was inquiring how many I wanted and told him it was just for myself, to go with a chop, and thought perhaps eight would do, if they were large ones. When

I am more used to shopping for myself I shall know in a flash, but at present I am rather feeling my way.

He is one of those sandy-haired young men, always trying to do six things at once. 'Not up there, Fred,' he shouted. 'They're under the caulies. What did you want, then?'

'About eight, I think,' I began, but broke off because he was telling a lady that the lettuces she was fingering were fresh in today. Then he took fourpence from a thrustful woman who came up with a lemon, and began to shovel up vast quantities of sprouts in a scoop.

'Got a sack?' he asked me.

'Good heavens!' I said. 'Are those for me? All I wanted –'

'Make up your mind,' he said. 'Eight pound, you *said*. If it's for Mrs Odding,' he added, speaking over his shoulder to a girl in a white overall, 'she has the Cos.'

I began to lose patience with these constant unmannerly interpolations. 'I do not care tuppence, young man,' I said warmly, 'whether Mrs Odding has the Cos – or the flu either, for that matter. All I want is a little civility, and some sprouts.'

One of those odd silences fell over the shop while I was speaking, and it may be that a sudden consciousness that heads were turning in my direction put me momentarily off my guard. At any rate, in making way for a woman who came bustling past me with a push-chair, I took an incautious pace backwards and fouled the carrot rack. It is absurd to have such an insecure structure in a busy shop. After all, one can move about perfectly freely in a fishmonger's without bringing a hundredweight of haddock about one's ears; or in a hat shop or chemist's for that matter, *mutatis mutandis*, now that they no longer pile up sponges and loofahs in inadequate wire baskets. There ought to be more consideration and common sense. Ironmongers hang their surplus shovels and brooms and so on from the ceiling, and though that might not do in every case it shows what can be achieved by the exercise of a little imagination. At Burgrove Preparatory School the boys' bowler hats (for travelling, etc.) used to be kept piled up on a shelf at elbow level, but soon after my arrival there as Assistant Matheatical Master they were moved to a high cupboard out of reach – another case in point.

Everybody was very kind and helpful, but in the end I left without buying any sprouts and went, almost directly, to Gooch's for tobacco. He also sells walking-sticks, though I don't quite see the connexion. Something to do with the open air perhaps, unless briar was once used for both – I mean for pipes as well as for walking-sticks, or rather the other way round. But that hardly seems likely.

Miss Edge was in Gooch's and shook her finger at me in a way I do not much admire.

'What's this I hear about you pelting Mrs Odding with carrots, Mr Wentworth?' she said immediately.

The speed with which gossip, and highly inaccurate gossip at that, flies about a small place like Fenport still astonishes me, though I have been there six months or more now and ought to be finding my feet. It was bad enough in a Common Room, but here!

'Pelting Mrs Odding!' I cried, hardly able to believe my ears. 'Why, I – '

'With carrots,' she repeated, nodding. 'Over at Wrightson's. And calling her names, by all accounts. I didn't even know you knew her.'

'I do *not*,' I replied, colouring up. 'What is more, Miss Edge, sorry as I am to scotch so succulent a snake at birth, she was not even in the shop at the time. I merely – '

'Oh, Mr Wentworth!' she said. 'Behind her back! That *was* naughty.'

'One does not pelt people with carrots behind their backs,' I began heatedly; but noticing that Mrs French and her little boy had entered the shop and seemed to be listening I broke off and asked for an ounce of Richmond Curly Cut.

'Five,' the girl said.

'No, one,' I corrected her.

'Five shillings,' said Old Gooch, intervening. 'Just gone up.'

Five shillings! And I can remember when it was seven-pence. Still, there it is. One must move with the times or go under, as happened to a poor old friend of mine when haircuts went up to one-and-six. After all, it is cheaper to hav one's teeth out now than it was in the old days, so that on thing balances another up to a point.

Miss Edge was nowhere to be seen when I turned t continue our conversation, and I made my way home in thoughtful frame of mind. It is idle to concern oneself over much with the small contretemps of every day; gossip-monge will make mountains out of molehills, do what one will. Non the less it distressed me to think that this Mrs Odding might b led to believe that I had spoken rudely about her, if (as wa more than probable) some garbled version of the incident wer to reach her ears. It would be better, I decided – rightly I sti think – to ring the lady up and explain the whole thing quit simply, before Miss Edge or anybody else had a chance t upset her with ill-natured tittle-tattle. But of course that mean that I must waste no time at all.

There is only one Odding in the book – it is an unusua name, I think – so there was no difficulty about that.

'Odding here,' said a man's voice, when I got through.

'I have just come from the greengrocer's,' I explained, '– that is, I wonder, could I speak to Mrs Odding, please?'

'For you,' I heard him say. 'Chap from the greengrocer's Got a mouthful of potatoes to get rid of, by the sound of it.'

If a lifetime's schoolmastering has taught me nothing els (as it certainly has), I have at last learned to disregard trivia rudenesses. Of course, in this instance, I was no doubt no intended to overhear what was said, but I could not help wondering whether Mr Odding has ever paused to conside what his *own* voice may sound like when distorted by th telephone.

'Yais? What then? Mrs Odding spiks,' another voice said

'Oh, Mrs Odding,' I said – with rather a sinking heart, to tell the truth – 'I am sorry to trouble you, but I just wanted to clear up a small matter, a silly little incident at the green – '

'Is arrived,' Mrs Odding said. 'He is come O.K. Beets and all.'

'Yes, yes,' I said. 'This is another matter. I happened to be in Wrightson's this afternoon when one of the assistants – '

'Is right?'

'Wrightson's, Mrs Odding. With a W, you know. One of the assistants, the sandy-haired one actually, mentioned that you preferred the Cos, the lettuce, you understand – '

'Alwais,' she said firmly. 'Never the other. It is becoss of the vind.'

'I see. Well – '

'Up she comes, else. With Cos, no. If he is not Cos, back she goes. You know me?'

'No, Mrs Odding,' I said. 'That is what I wanted to explain.' I did not, as a matter of fact, want to do anything of the kind. I am not in any sense a Little Englander: some of my best friend are Balts and Slovenes and so on; and I am well aware of the importance of reaching a close understanding with people who have not had the same advantages as we have – or perhaps one ought to say not the same kind of advantages, to avoid the risk of misunderstanding. But, really! When it comes to clearing up a silly little affair in a greengrocer's one would rather have to do with one's own kidney.

'Mrs Odding,' I went on, speaking slowly and distinctly, 'I simply rang up to ask you to take no notice of any stupid stories you may hear about a trifling incident in the greengrocer's this afternoon. When I tell you that people are already going about saying that I pelted you with carrots, Mrs Odding, at a time when, as you and I know perfectly well – '

'Here, I've had enough of this,' said Mr Odding's voice. 'Who the devil are you? And what do you mean by trying to frighten my wife with a lot of damn balderdash about carrots? Ringing up in the middle of tea and scaring a woman out of her wits after all she's been through these last months – '

I allow no one to take that tone with me, least of all when I am attempting to make an apology.

'My name is Wentworth,' I said coldly, 'and I would have you know that – '

'Aha!' he said. 'So *that's* it.' And rang off.

Two minutes later the phone rang again, and I supposed it would be this man, Odding, come to his senses and anxious to explain himself. But it turned out to be Harcutt, a solicitor whom I have met once or twice at the library and so on.

'I say, Wentworth,' he said, 'speaking as a friend, is it true you called Miss Edge a succulent snake at the chemist's this afternoon?'

One really has no patience with this kind of folly.

'If you are thinking of joining the Old Women's Scandal-mongering Society, Harcutt,' I suggested, 'you had better try to get *some* of your facts right. In the first place, Miss Edge and I met not at the chemist's but at Gooch's.'

'That certainly alters the situation,' he said.

'And secondly, I called her no such thing. I should have thought you knew me well enough by this time. The amount of petty gossip and trouble-making that goes on in this place – '

'Well, keep your hair on, Wentworth,' he said – an expression I have always disliked. 'I was only joking.'

'And while we are about it,' I told him, 'here is a further bit of information for you. I did not throw carrots at Mrs Odding in the greengrocer's either.'

'You didn't?'

'No.'

'Then why mention it?'

'Because I have no doubt that it is all over the village by now.'

'Wait a minute, Wentworth,' he said. 'Are you suggesting that things have reached such a pitch that the fact that you *didn't* throw carrots at somebody is red-hot news?'

'Oh, go and boil yourself, Harcutt,' I said. He is a good chap in many ways, but I was not in the mood for that kind of schoolboy facetiousness. All this fuss over buying a few sprouts, and even then I did not get any.

I took up the dictionary after supper, to calm my mind, and looked up 'briar'. Apparently they don't make pipes from the prickly kind, but from the root of a sort of heath, which makes the connexion between tobacco and walking-sticks all the more mysterious. The word comes from the French *bruyère*, to my surprise. I had always thought it a kind of cheese.

Brains Trust

e Conservative Association holds from time to time what
y call a Brains Trust. St Mark's Hall is not a very cheerful
ce for it, in many ways; the walls are dark green and tend
sweat, and of course rows and rows of rush-bottomed chairs
er suggest cosiness. Still, people come. I dare say they like to
our local M.P., Sir Arnold Bantry, who is always on the
nel', and other notabilities from Fenport and West Acre
l even farther afield. It makes an evening, as Mrs Wheeler
s it.

little thought, when I first strolled along to St Mark's six
nths or so ago, that I should one day be 'on the panel'
self. But Mrs Dalrymple has been most pressing. 'Every-
ly's tired of these endless barristers and journalists,' she told
'We need fresh blood, a new outlook. Do say yes.' At first
lemurred. One does not like to stand in the way of the
unger people. Besides, my knowledge of the world is to some
ent departmentalized and, though I make it my business to
e a lively interest in everything that goes on around me, I
ght well be floored by a question on, let us say, the Middle
st oil situation – or as I told Mrs Dalrymple – anything
ut marital relationships, which I have never had. However,
entirely misunderstood my point.

There's nothing to be frightened of, Mr Wentworth,' she
d. 'The audience are very friendly and the Chairman will
p you all he can – Sidney Megrim is so good – and see you
ely through those "beginner's nerves".'

The idea that I, after a lifetime's schoolmastering, might be
rmed at the thought of facing a roomful of middle-aged

ladies in a tuppeny-ha'penny place like Fenport was really
much. I made a somewhat emphatic reply, which M
Dalrymple took as an acceptance, so that I found myself cc
mitted before I had really considered the matter fully. 'N
Thursday, then, at 8 p.m.,' she said gaily. 'And the very l
of luck.'

The short notice made me wonder whether somebody
had fallen out at the last moment, and the suspicion beca
a virtual certainty when the Chairman introduced the me
bers of the panel to the audience, getting my name right l
adding that I was an authority on Elizabethan Drama a
had been in my day a well-known amateur actor. No do
somebody had forgotten to alter the notes given to him ab
the original panellist. It is all in the day's work, but even s
'In my day', if you please. One is not a hundred and fifty
have never acted, as it happens, but if I had I dare say I co
act as well today as ever I did. Better, very likely, with all
added experience of life and character and so on that the ye
bring. Everybody clapped politely, as they do at these affa
and the Chairman read out the first question before I ha
chance to put the matter right.

It was about woman's proper place being in the home a
Sir Arnold, who spoke first, made the apt point that it was
Conservative policy to encourage women to devote to th
homes the time and energy demanded by their proud positic
as wives and mothers, while at the same time developing in
larger world outside those public and civic qualities up
which so much depended. He then criticized the Socialists
their attitude to the Early Closing Act of (if I rememl
rightly) 1922, and was reminded of an amusing incident
which he missed an important appointment in Lond
through some misunderstanding about spaghetti. I forget h
he linked it up, but it was all very skilfully done and show
how a practised speaker can turn the most unlikely subject i
grist for his mill.

A Mr Philip Tallboys said he agreed with every word t
Member had said, and had little to add except it was no g
saying that woman's proper place was in the home unless y

first made sure that she *had* a home to take her proper place in. The Conservatives had no reason to be ashamed of their record in providing homes for the people. He is a chartered accountant, with a habit of slouching down in his chair and tapping his finger-tips together that struck me as a shade patronizing at a public meeting of this kind. Miss Gorman, on the other hand, who followed him with an interesting account of her life in a biological laboratory, leaned right forwards with her hands clasping her bag and described the 'worthwhileness' (to use her own phrase) of dissecting water-beetles and so on with an eagerness to which the front row of Fenport housewives were slow to respond. Or so I thought. It is a capital mistake to try to win sympathy by over-emphasis. Let the facts speak for themselves – such at least was my method when teaching geometry at Burgrove – instead of repeatedly urging their importance and interest.

While Miss Gorman was speaking I caught the eye of a man about four rows back who was putting a sweet of some kind in his mouth. Old habits die hard and I gave him a sharp look. I suppose there is no definite rule about eating at public meetings, but it would look very odd if those on the platform started putting toffees in their mouths, and what is sauce for the goose ought surely, as a matter of ordinary politeness, to be sauce for the gander. At any rate the man I caught at it clearly felt uneasy, for he gave a little cough and put his hand up to his mouth again – an old trick, designed to make one think that that was what he was doing the first time. Thereafter, whenever I glanced in his direction he instantly stopped chewing and stared straight ahead with rigid jaws. It was annoying to be unable to tell the silly fellow that a man with my training could see through a dozen better dodges than that. I remember a boy called Mason who took the rubber out of the metal holder on the end of his pencil and substituted pieces of mint humbug, cut to fit. He is an aeroplane designer now, they tell me, and putting his ingenuity, one hopes, to more worthwhile ends. But he very nearly fooled me at the time.

I mention this small incident only to explain why my attention was momentarily distracted when the Chairman called my name.

'Eh? What's that?' I asked.

'We are hoping,' he said amid some laughter, 'that you would have something to say on this question.'

'What question is that?'

'We have been discussing,' the Chairman said, with a long-suffering air that rather nettled me, 'whether woman's proper place is in the home.'

'Have you, indeed,' I replied. 'I was under the impression that you had been discussing whether the proper place for water-beetles was the Conservative Party.' This sally, which was of course intended, in part at least, to be in jocular vein, was very well received by the audience. Sir Arnold, however, saw fit to take offence.

'We certainly get all sorts at our meetings,' he remarked.

'It is quite clear, at any rate,' put in Miss Gorman, 'that the proper place for a woman is not Mr *Wentworth's* home.'

'I entirely agree,' I said. 'As I happen to be a bachelor, it would be most *im*proper.'

'That is a state of affairs that could easily be remedied,' the Chairman pointed out, when the laughter had died down. 'Perhaps Miss Gorman would co-operate?'

'Oh, I'm afraid my time is very much taken up with my water-beetles, which Mr Wentworth seems so much to despise,' Miss Gorman said, with a rather tight-lipped smile. 'Somebody else must accept the honour.'

'No room for just one more?' Tallboys asked.

I enjoy the cut and thrust of debate as much as any man, but there is a point, a very definite point, at which good-humoured raillery ends and impertinence begins. Miss Coombes, who looked after the boys' vests and so on at Burgrove, put it very well, I remember, when she said 'Anyone can be clever, Etheridge, but it takes a gentleman to be courteous.' Though I said nothing, some of the annoyance I felt may very well have shown in my face. At any rate, the man in the fourth row, in whose direction I happened to be looking, hastily whipped his handkerchief up to his mouth and

unless I am very much mistaken ejected whatever he was eating and put it into his pocket. Thereafter, I was glad to see he
paid close attention to what was being said, and once or twice
nodded his head to show agreement with some observation of
my own. I know the type from of old.

A man like Tallboys, with a hide three inches thick, has to
be handled differently. It is best, as a rule, to ignore them; and
that is what I did. The Chairman in any case had gone on to
the next question, which concerned our relations with the
United States. Miss Gorman said that the future of the world
depended on a close accord between the English-speaking
peoples, and with this we were all agreed. Then we discussed
juvenile delinquency, a subject on which I suppose I can claim
to speak with some authority. Not, naturally, that there was
anything serious of that kind at Burgrove, but boys are very
much alike the world over and only those who have spent a
lifetime in their company can hope to have a close understanding of their problems. I said that provided young people were
brought up in the right way, taught to fear God and be honour-
able and straightforward, tell the truth and play the game in
the widest sense of the phrase, we need have no fear that they
would grow up in the right way. The audience took this very
well, I think, and Sir Arnold backed me up by saying that a
good home was the important thing. Miss Gorman talked
about glands and suchlike hocus-pocus, and Tallboys said he
did not think a boy was any the worse for stealing a few apples
when the policeman wasn't looking. If that was how he spent
his own boyhood, he is not, in my opinion, much of an
advertisement for apple-stealing, but of course I did not say
so. I leave cheap scores to others. The Chairman summed up,
neatly enough, by saying that the panel seemed to be agreed
on the whole that the younger generation would be all right
provided they were taught to behave themselves.

After that we discussed interplanetary travel and mixed
marriages and the best present to give a man on his fiftieth
birthday. Then the Chairman announced that there were five
more minutes to go and asked if any member of the audience
had a question he or she would like to put. At once a woman

got up and asked the extraordinary question 'Can the pane
explain why there is no Request Stop at the bottom of Penfiel
Road, and isn't it high time something was done about it?'

Well!

I suppose it is natural, in a way, that people's small loca
concerns should be of more interest to them than some of th
questions, many of them of fundamental importance, we ha
been discussing. But the immediate quickening of interest too
me, I must confess, by surprise.

'Quite right, Mrs Burfitt,' somebody called out. 'Fou
hundred yards if it's an inch my little girl has to walk – '

'It's the shopping,' a thin woman in a beret explained. 'Yo
don't want to trudge right up Elm Street with a heavy basket

'I hardly think – ' the Chairman said.

'Take Friday. There was a good half-dozen of us in all tha
rain, and it isn't as if you could always take your overshoe:
You'd think they could do *something*.'

'*Didn't* it come down, Mrs Enticott! I saw you there, bu
not to speak to, being in the back, and I said to my husban
"The poor thing *will* get wet, I told him – " '

'It's the same with the footpath back of the common,' :
bald-headed man complained, without troubling to rise to hi
feet. 'You could break a leg in one of those pot-holes. It's al
very well for the panel to come here and talk about mixe
marriages and satellites and that, but what I'd like to know i
when is something going to be done about the disgraceful stat
of some of our public paths?'

'Hear! Hear!' said several voices.

What astonished me was the Chairman's acquiescence ir
this absurd situation. He seemed perfectly content to sit bacl
and allow the meeting to degenerate into a disorderly hubbub
Of course in a way it was no business of mine, but when :
young woman got up and demanded two additional har
tennis courts in the Recreation Ground, or some such nonsense
I really could stand it no longer.

'This is not a meeting of the Rural District Counci
madam,' I said. 'The panel is here, if the Chairman will allov

ne to say so, to answer questions of general interest, not to
repair footpaths or insist on additional Request Stops – '

'But a stop at the bottom of Penfield Road *is* of general
interest,' interrupted Miss Gorman, in what I am afraid was
a rather obvious attempt to curry favour. 'It is certainly a
matter of great interest to *me*.'

'In that case,' I replied, unable to repress a touch of sarcasm
– a weapon that I am normally very loth to use, 'I shall of
course make it my business to take the matter up with the bus
company at the earliest possible opportunity.'

'And don't forget the footpath,' somebody called out.

These people seem to think that, just because one is on a
platform, one has nothing better to do than see to all the trivial
problems they are too lazy to work out for themselves. Really,
one might as well be back at school.

One Thing after Another

Word has got round that I am taking up the matter of the Penfield Road bus stop. Mrs Wheeler went out of her way to congratulate me about it this morning after church.

'We need somebody of energy and initiative in this place, Mr Wentworth,' she told me. 'There is so much to be done. It is splendid to know that you are going to interest yourself in our small concerns.'

It is absurd that a chance remark, made in a spirit of irony at a so-called 'Brains Trust', should be taken up in this literal way. But what is one to do? Mrs Wheeler would rightly have felt very rudely rebuffed had I replied that I had no intention of doing anything of the kind. Besides, I suppose in a way it is just the opportunity I have been looking for to give a helping hand here and there in Fenport. When one joins a community one has no right, even in retirement, to sit back with folded hands and expect others to do the work. 'Heaven helps those that helps theirselves' is an old adage of my nurse's that comes to mind.

I was revolving in my mind the opening phrases of a letter to the West Acre and District Transport Company, when I was hailed by Miss Stephens from the Bank. She is petite and does not, I am sure, dye her hair. Some women have a natural bronze that grows a little paler at the roots.

'Oh, Mr Wentworth,' she began in her breathless way, 'of course we hardly know each other, and I do hope you will forgive me, but the fact of the matter is it's the Dramatic Society. We are doing *The Linden Tree*, you see, it's a Priestley of course, and the old Professor – he's out of date, if you

iember, and *won't* give up despite his wife's longing to get
ay from it all – '

But, Miss Stephens,' I interrupted gently, 'I am rather at a
. I shall of course be delighted to take a ticket when the
e comes – '

But we want you to *act*, Mr Wentworth,' she cried. 'It's a
t that's simply made for you. So gentle, and yet so firm. I
just see you, in the big scene with Mrs Linden – '

naturally supposed at first that she was pulling my leg.
But after a while as she prattled on, I realized that she
ously imagined I might be persuaded to go on the stage in
it of half the people in Fenport and involve myself in this
ie with Mrs Linden, whoever she might be. At my age! So
ized the first opportunity to tell her that I had never acted
ny life, and that I feared I was a little old to begin now.

She opened her eyes very wide indeed.

But, Mr Wentworth!' she said. 'I know that you used ...
ore half the crowned heads of Europe, Mr Megrim told

Oh, Megrim!' I said.

saw at once that this, like the bus stop business, was
ther result of Sidney Megrim's stupidly inept handling of
Brains Trust meeting. The next thing would be, no doubt,
t somebody would ask me to give a talk to the Literary and
ating Club on Elizabethan Drama.

Let me assure you, Miss Stephens,' I said, 'that any stories
ut my having once been an actor are quite unfounded.
art from one occasion in the old days when I dressed up as
her Christmas for an end-of-term concert, I can truthfully
– '

And what are two of my parishioners hatching up together
inst me now?' cried the vicar, coming up unexpectedly
n behind. He has a way of taking one by the elbow that, in
not of his cloth, I should be inclined to resent. 'Something
ny detriment, I'll be bound.'

Somers is a good man, with no high-church nonsense about
, but perhaps rather roguish for his years.

You are barking up the wrong tree, Vicar,' I told him,

seeking unsuccessfully to free myself. 'I was simply explainir
to Miss Stephens that, though I have dressed up as Fath
Christmas in my time — '

'The very man,' he interrupted. 'The very man! Now th
poor old Witherby has been laid to rest. Miss Stephens, yo
shall persuade him. Four o'clock at the vicarage, on Decemb
the 20th. Vestments provided by the parish. Splendid, sple
did. You have no idea, Wentworth, how difficult it is nowada
to get the right sort of person to take an interest in our sm;
doings.'

'Well, really — ' I began.

'Mr Wentworth is thinking of joining our Dramatic Society
Miss Stephens said. 'Just for a small part, perhaps, until v
see how he gets on. We mustn't ask *too* much of him, mu
we?'

'Mine is no more than a walking-on-part, as we say,' sa
the vicar. 'Just a word here and there to the kiddies. A pat c
the head, perhaps. You have patted heads in your time, e:
Wentworth? Four o'clock then, on the 20th of next month.'

'I very much fear,' I said — but he had darted off in h
impetuous way to accost a young couple with a dachshun<
and I turned to find Miss Stephens laughing gaily at me.

'*What* a breezy Christian it is,' she exclaimed. 'I always fe
I ought to hold my skirts down when he's about.'

I dug the ferrule of my umbrella into the ground, at a lo
for a reply.

'And hold my hat on tight and so on, I mean,' she went o
with a becoming blush. 'That *was* naughty of you, about hii
barking up the wrong tree. I very nearly burst right out.'

'Naughty?' I said. 'In what way?'

'Don't pretend you don't know everybody calls him Frisk
Fido. I should think he knows it himself, very likely.'

'Oh, that,' I said. 'Oh well.' It was the first I had heard c
it, as a matter of fact, but I cannot say I was greatly surprisec
The more I see of life in this neighbourhood, the more it seem
to me to resemble life in a boys' preparatory school. The gossi
and childishness of it all, and now nicknames for the vicar

he only difference in a way is that there is practically no
scipline.

We had quite a pleasant talk, until our ways parted at the
ina shop. Miss Stephens is an amusing little thing, and I
ould be glad to help her, within reason. But there are limits.
do not think I have committed myself about her absurd play-
ting suggestion, though of course, up to a point, it might be
hew experience. We shall see.

is odd to remember that a little time ago I was complaining
a lack of useful employment here in Fenport. And now here
am, practically rushed off my feet with this Penfield Road
usiness and rehearsals for Miss Stephens's Dramatic Society
arting on Wednesday (it is really impossible to refuse so
essing a lady), not to mention the vicar's Children's Party,
ough that of course is not for a few weeks yet. Then there is
e Vice-Presidency of the Football Club – I mean I have still
settle whether to accept the honour at a guinea a year or
nd them a gracefully-worded refusal. All these things mount
).

'Don't you go and do too much, Mr Wentworth,' Mrs
etton said to me only this morning as I was on my way out
the tool-shed to straighten things up in there. 'You're too
nd-hearted by far. You want to take it easy, your time of
e, not run this way and that for a pack of women.' She is an
ccellent creature, but a little inclined to treat me as though I
ere an elderly invalid. 'That Miss Stephens,' she added, and
ould I think have said more, had I not shown by my manner
at I had work to do. I do not believe in encouraging gossip,
owever well intentioned.

I keep my bicycle in the tool-shed, together with the mow-
g machine and other odds and ends. This is inconvenient at
nes, because of the way things have of catching in things
hen you want them – or rather when you don't. I mean
hen you don't want the things they catch in, naturally, and
is these for some tiresome reason that generally come out first
hen you pull. Besides, it is bad for the spokes. A lot of old
aint-tins and so on were left behind by the last occupant into

the bargain, and the place needs a thorough tidy. I hate a
thing slipshod. The School Museum was in my charge
Burgrove for a number of years, so I am not without exp
ence of arranging a number of diverse objects to the
advantage in a narrow space.

The right way to begin is to clear everything out first,
this I proceeded to do (not, for reasons that I have explai
without some difficulty). I shall never understand why
predecessor here needed so much garden hose. It is awkw
stuff at the best of times, and really, for the small lawn
two rose beds which are all I have here, one would h
thought forty feet or so would be enough. I very much do
as a matter of fact, whether he ever used it at all; parts of
middle section have clearly, to judge by the cobwebs al
been entangled in an old wooden rake for many years. At
rate, after a tug or two, I decided that the only thing to do
to unthread the hose carefully from end to end, to diseng
it, that is to say, from the various articles with which it
become entangled. These latter could then be remo
seriatim.

To my astonishment, the hose appeared to have no e
whichever way I traced it, and it was while trying to follo
double loop through the framework of a deck-chair tha
somehow got the handle of a pair of edging shears up the
leg of my trousers. I should not ordinarily note down the det
of so mundane an operation as tidying out a shed, but th
has been a lot of exaggerated gossip in the village – *nothin*
too trivial, it seems, for some people – and in justice to my
I wish to explain, quite briefly, what happened next.

Anyone who has tried to trace an unrolled garden hose,
a tangled fishing cast for that matter, to its source knows t
it is essential at no time to lose touch. The eye is not to
depended upon. The entire length must be followed *by ha*
for otherwise it is all too easy to reverse one's direction
knowingly where two loops intersect and thus arrive back
one's starting point. For this reason I was obliged to force
way *through* rather than to go *round* the deck-chair, and b
stroke of ill-luck the serrated, or notched, leg of the cha

/hich happened to be uppermost, swung over on its pivots and rapped the upper part of my body. At the same time the point f the shears became jammed rather awkwardly in the lower ramework – of the chair, that is – and in attempting to preerve my balance I inadvertently gave a sharpish tug to the nose (of which, I must repeat, I could not let go without hrowing all my trouble to the winds) and brought down a quantity of sacking and old dahlia tubers from a shelf above ny head. I was temporarily blinded. But for that I should ertainly not have made what turned out to be a false move.

I suppose it may have been two or three minutes later that I heard footsteps on the gravel path outside. Not wishing to be nterrupted I kept quite still, and it was with some irritation hat I heard Mrs Bretton call out, rather gruffly, 'Here's Miss ›tephens wants to see you, Mr Wentworth.' Still, there was nothing to be done, and a moment later I could sense that Miss ›tephens was standing in the doorway.

'I'm so sorry to bother you when you are busy,' she began. Then her voice died away. 'Oh my God, Mrs Bretton!' she cried. (I suppose it is the modern way, but I do *not* like it in a woman.) 'There's something hanging up in the corner.'

The truth was that in an instinctive effort to free myself by lipping backwards through the framework of the chair and at the same time *shrugging* it, if I make myself clear, upwards, I had caught the leg-rung, by a million-to-one chance, on some nail or projection in the wall. Movement of any kind was now painful, if not positively dangerous, and it was while quietly hinking out the next step that I had become aware that I had a visitor.

'It is perfectly all right, Miss Stephens,' I said, to reassure her. 'I was looking for the end of the hose.'

'Goodness, you gave me a shock,' she said. 'It's hanging lown your back.'

'Aha!' I said. 'It must have been hidden among the dahlias.'

'So are you, you poor thing,' Miss Stephens said, coming – ery expertly, I must say – to my assistance.

The upshot of all this is that I have practically promised to ake a part in her play. Apparently, a Wally Bishop is going abroad, and they are desperate for somebody to act the part of Lockhart, whoever *he* may be. To tell the truth, I was not in the best of tempers – nobody likes to be interrupted in the middle of a worthwhile task – and the quickest way to settle the matter seemed to be to say yes.

'In that case,' I said, 'I suppose – very well. By all means, if you wish it. Yes.'

'You *darling*!' Miss Stephens said. Of course, I know that it means nothing, among stage people, but all the same on was glad that Mrs Bretton had gone to get her husband's lunch

The first performance is to be on December 20th, apparently. I have a feeling that I already have some engagement for that date, but Miss Stephens says it doesn't matter. I don't know, I'm sure, whether I have been altogether wise.

The Penfield Road Affair

man named Willis, who is something to do with the Gas
ompany I believe, called about the H-bomb this morning. He
ld me that sheep were eating grass coated with Strontium 90,
some such number, and wanted me to protest about it.

'This is all a little bit outside my province,' I told him. I
how nothing about sheep, and was in any case rather busy.

'Is the extermination of the whole human race outside your
rovince, then?' he asked.

'It is certainly more than I have time for this morning,' I
id, ignoring the rudeness of his manner. 'At the moment I
ave my hands full with this business of a Request Stop at the
ottom of Penfield Road. Perhaps, while you are here, you
ould care to join in a protest against the intransigent attitude
the bus company? Only a few days ago, I am told – '

He seemed to be a man without any sense of proportion.
Penfield Road!' he cried. 'A fat lot it will matter whether the
uses stop at Penfield Road or anywhere else when there's
obody left to ride in them and the whole of Europe is a
esolate waste. It's people like you, with their noses buried in
heir own petty little local affairs, that are bringing the world
the brink of destruction. Can't you realize that already sea-
eed is being dredged up with point nought six of a fatal dose
radiation in it? And you talk about bus stops!'

I am not the man to be hectored on my own doorstep.

'Listen to me, young man,' I said. 'When I was your age
here were plenty of people going about saying that the end of
e world was at hand. They used to hold meetings, I re-
ember, with the slogan "Millions Now Living Will Never
ie". A fine state we should all have been in if I had listened

to them and decided it was not worth while to go on teachi
my boys trigonometry. Get on with your own job, my lad, a
leave sheep and seaweed to wiser heads.' For two pins I wor
have told him to get his hair cut and take his bicycle-clips
before calling uninvited at strange houses. I did, in fact, s
something of the kind, more or less *sotto voce*, and he we
away muttering.

I had meant to get a strong letter off to the bus compa
(or the *Advertiser* perhaps would be better), but this Wi
interview unsettled me and after thinking things over for
hour or two I set off to change a book at the library. M
Wheeler was there, half-way up a ladder, and we chatted
a while.

'I feel like Romeo and Juliet,' she said. 'Why not come a
have dinner one evening, Mr Wentworth? On Friday wee
One or two people will be there whom you might like to me
if you haven't met them already.'

'I'm sure I shall be delighted to meet them even if I *ha*
met them already,' I said politely. I had not intended any jo
but Mrs Wheeler began to laugh so I joined in.

'That would depend, wouldn't it?' she said. 'Suppose
asked Mr Willis?'

'Willis!' I said. 'You mean the gas man!'

'He says you threw his bicycle-clips in his face. I must s
it doesn't sound very likely, but he *did* seem angry. Of cour
he did not say it to me, but they were outside Gooch's just n
and I couldn't very well help hearing. Then that m
Odding –'

'Odding?'

'Yes. They were talking, you see. Odding said nothi
would surprise him. He said you rang his wife up the other d
and threatened to pelt her with carrots. There was somethi
else, but I had my shopping to do, and of course –'

'This is getting beyond a joke,' I broke in angrily. 'If the
two men are getting together to spread slanderous stories abc
me I shall certainly take action. The whole thing is a mar
nest. I simply rang up Mrs Odding to explain that if she hea
any silly stories about my – about carrots being thrown at h

at the greengrocer's it was all a misunderstanding. She is unfortunately an Estonian – '

'But, Mr Wentworth, surely even an Estonian would know
whether she was or was not being pelted with carrots. I mean
if it wasn't true, I don't quite see – '

'Exactly,' I said. 'The carrots have been trumped up against
me by ill-disposed gossips. There were a few on the floor, not
more than a few, and nobody was hurt. Actually, the whole
thing started with a lettuce.'

'You threw a lettuce at Mrs Odding?'

'I neither threw, nor threatened to throw, anything at anybody, Mrs Wheeler. I merely gave vent to an expression at the
greengrocer's – '

'Muriel!' Mrs Wheeler called out suddenly. 'Mr Wentworth is telling me how he gave vent to an expression at the
greengrocer's.'

I had not noticed Miss Stephens come into the library. She
now joined us with an 'Oh, do tell!' and the two ladies listened
sympathetically while I gave a short account of the circumstances that had led me to make a hasty remark in Wrightson's
shop about Mrs Odding's order for lettuces, and how my
attempt to apologize to the woman on the telephone had been
misinterpreted by her fool of a husband. 'The whole thing is a
storm in a tea-cup,' I ended.

'I don't suppose you really threw Willis's cycle-clips in his
face either,' Mrs Wheeler commented.

'Oh *no*?' Miss Stephens cried. 'Mr Wentworth, you really
are!'

I explained that the man had no doubt been speaking
figuratively. 'I may be old-fashioned,' I said, 'but I would
never dream of going to anybody's front door without removing my bicycle-clips, and I do not expect people to come to
mine without removing theirs. All the same, I should have said
nothing, of course, if the man had been civil. Standing there
lecturing me about seaweed and decrying the Request Stop,
when I am old enough to be his father, though I am bound to
say that I should have to be a *great* deal older before I would
dream – however, that is neither here nor there. The man was

uncivil, and I sent him away with a flea in his ear, as my old
nurse used to say.'

Both ladies were blowing their noses, and there was a short
silence.

'I'm sure he richly deserved it,' Mrs Wheeler said. 'He was
rude about the – about the Request Stop, you say?'

'I thought he would be better employed in joining me in a
protest about the Penfield Road business than in badgering
people with a lot of nonsense about radioactive sheep. "Get
your hair cut," I told him, "and leave all that tomfoolery to
wiser heads".'

'That settled *him*, I should think,' Mrs Wheeler said. 'But
I *am* so glad you are taking the Request Stop so seriously. And
what a splendid idea to organize a protest!'

'Hardly that. Hardly that, dear lady,' I said. 'I am merely
writing a letter to the *Advertiser*, which I think will do some
good.'

'I certainly mustn't miss *that*,' Miss Stephens said.

Their interest and enthusiasm encouraged me to go straight
home and write a fairly stiff letter to the local paper, without
further delay. It will make the West Acre and Fenport Transport Company sit up, I fancy.

This Penfield Road bus-stop affair is becoming more of a
nuisance than it is worth. A day or two after posting my letter
to the *Advertiser* it occurred to me to walk out and see the
actual terrain, what was involved in the way of distance,
between existing stops, etc. 'Get out into the field, Wentworth,'
my old C.O. used to say to me in the last war, and though I
never quite became used to being spoken to as if I were a horse,
I am sure his advice was sound. An ounce of knowledge is
worth a deal of theory, as they say.

It was a considerable shock to me to find that there is already
a Request Stop at Penfield Road. I can only suppose that the
bus company had got wind of the fact that the matter was
being taken up by someone who was not likely to be put off by
excuses and evasions, and had decided to anticipate what they
knew to be an unanswerable demand. I felt very badly let

wn, and my first thought was, of course, to withdraw the
ter I had written to the *Advertiser*. This meant fourpence in
telephone kiosk which I can ill afford.

'I wrote you a letter the day before yesterday,' I said as soon
I was through. 'About the Request Stop at Penfield – '

'Do you want Basting?' a voice said.

'Certainly not,' I replied. 'I wish the letter to be withdrawn
mediately. It must not appear.'

'You want the Editor then,' the voice said. 'Only he's out.'

'Who is that?' I asked sharply. 'I must speak to the Editor.
his is a matter of the utmost – '

'Mr Basting's gone, see? If it's about the letter, it's in. This
Partridge 'ere, the boy, and it'll be out Friday.'

'No, no,' I said. 'It must come out *now*! The letter must not
pear. I am speaking from Penfield Road, and the fact is that
bus stop has recently been installed. That being so – '

'We knew that, o' course,' the boy said.

'Then naturally you will not print my letter, which was
ritten in ignorance of the facts.'

'It's in,' he repeated. 'On the machines. "It'll stir up cor-
spondence, anyway," Mr Basting said. "There'll be plenty
f people glad enough to point out the error," he said. He said
e don't get a letter putting its foot in it right up to the neck
ery week, he said. "And what's more," he said – '

Never, even in my schoolmastering days (except perhaps in
e matter of the changing-room pegs in Poole's time) have I
et so utterly irresponsible an attitude. 'Listen to me, Part-
dge,' I said. 'I think you are mistaking your man. You may
ll your Editor from me that if my letter is printed I shall not
esitate to write him another, which he will not like. He has
o business to include correspondence, written as I say, in
norance of the facts – '

'Look,' the boy had the impertinence to reply, 'if we cut out
tters just because they were written in ignorance of the facts,
e wouldn't *have* no correspondence. "Bung it in," Mr Basting
id to me – '

I was not prepared, of course, to listen to this kind of talk.
Bung it in,' indeed! Sometimes I wonder what the world is

coming to, when young flippertigibbets, scarcely out of the teens to judge by their voices, can speak in that strain to a m. old enough to have forgotten more than they ever learnt. this is what comes of trying to give a helping hand to the peop of this village they will soon find that they have a very differe kettle of fish to deal with. It is all very well to pester me to dre up as Father Christmas next December and have this extr ordinary scene with Mrs Linden, if that was the name, and this that and the other thing, but if all I am to get in return a lot of inaccurate gossip about throwing carrots, at *my* ag and now this trouble with the *Advertiser*, I might as well back to Burgrove and try to hammer a bit of sense into a lot boys who, with all their faults, never dreamed of using stro language in my presence. There is such a thing as flogging dead horse, as I shall tell them.

The Party at the Vicarage

It has been a trying day, and might well have ended in a contretemps. But as I have often found in life, difficulties and mishaps are there to be overcome, and if faced with calmness and common sense sometimes turn out to be all for the best. Looking back on it all, I cannot feel that there is anything to regret, though of course another year, before agreeing to give away the presents at the Vicarage Christmas Party, I shall make certain that it does not clash with the opening night of the Dramatic Society's play – assuming (as I am bold enough to do) that Miss Stephens will again ask me to take a part. Dashing from one engagement to another, for all the world as if I were a Prime Minister or some such functionary, is a bit too much of a good thing at my time of life.

Things would have run more smoothly, I dare say, but for a muddle over my Father Christmas outfit. This was no fault of mine, for I was in good time at the Vicarage and naturally expected to find everything ready for me there. It was quite a shock when Mrs Somers greeted me, almost before I had got my bicycle-clips off, with a cry of 'But where are your *things*?' She told me that they had been sent round to my house so that I could try them on, get used to the feel of the beard and so on – 'We always did that in poor Witherby's time,' she said, as though that had anything to do with it – and what she could *not* understand was how I had failed to see the parcel.

'Naturally I saw the parcel, Mrs Somers,' I replied. 'At least, I saw *a* parcel that somebody must have left on my doorstep when I was out. But I am afraid I am old-fashioned enough, when parcels come for me at this season, not to open them until Christmas Day.'

Mrs Somers threw up her hands in a gesture that, considering the circumstances, I found somewhat irritating. 'The children will be bitterly disappointed,' she said. 'We had hoped that you would be ready to greet them when they arrived, and – Oh dear! Here comes Mrs Thompson already with her two. *What* are we to do?'

Well, I have faced worse crises many a time in the old days, without losing my head as Mrs Somers seemed to have done. I shall not forget in a hurry the time the under-Matron came back from a wedding in a very strained state, and I had to make an immediate decision whether to send the boys out on a run or order them into the gymnasium for extra P.T. It would have been better, as it turned out, to send them for a run; but the important thing, as I explained to the Headmaster, was to get them out of the way quickly, not to stand about debating the pros and cons. I could not possibly know that Miss Vincent would herself go straight to the gym to sleep it off. There was the occasion, too, when the chapel organ became waterlogged on Confirmation Sunday – but there is no need to go into all that now. My point is that an old schoolmaster is not likely to be thrown out of his stride by a temporary hitch at a children's party.

'Surely, Mrs Somers,' I said quietly, 'it will be more effective if I arrive *after* the children are assembled? As though by sleigh. It will take me no more than twenty minutes to ride home, collect the parcel and return.'

'They will see you arriving,' she said. 'They are as sharp as needles.'

'It will be dark,' I replied. 'What is more, to be on the safe side, I will put on the costume before approaching the house. I do not see, in that case that it will matter even if – '

'Oh, Mr Wentworth!' she cried. 'Without a sack, and wheeling a bicycle! The children would be bitterly – '

'Then what do you suggest, madam?' I asked, very nearly at the end of my patience.

She bit her lip. 'Perhaps, if you wouldn't mind,' she said –

Here comes Mrs Whitney's little boy, in tears already – if you would come in by the side gate when you get back? Down the lane here, and up through the garden to the conservatory door. You would be out of sight from the front, you see, and we could give you the sack – '

'Give me the sack, eh?' I put in. 'There's gratitude for you!' But she was too fussed to appreciate the joke, and with an abrupt 'I must fly!' went off into the house.

I found when I got home that the parcel, mainly because of the top-boots, was too bulky to be carried on my bicycle, so there was nothing for it but to ride back to the Vicarage in full Father Christmas rig. The beard I could of course have strapped to the carrier or thrust into an inside pocket, but after some hesitation I put it on. It would be better, I thought, in case I were seen on the journey, not to be too readily recognizable.

I have had little or no experience of bicycling in fancy dress, and after one or two unsuccessful attempts to mount in the normal manner I realized that it would be necessary to pull the cloak up about my waist. I therefore gathered the skirts and had raised them with some difficulty as far as my knees when a voice called out 'Oh! Oh!', adding as it receded into the dusk, 'Time for another Request Stop agitation.' I could not see the face of the passer-by who made this senseless remark, but I have reason to believe that it was Willis, of the Gas Company, a man I have never liked. He has some bee in his bonnet about saving the world from annihilation, but would be better advised in my opinion to start by mending his manners. At any rate I made no reply and once I had learned the trick of turning the toes of my top boots outwards to avoid fouling the front mudguard was soon on my way. I dare say some of my Burgrove boys would have been surprised if they could have seen their old master pedalling along in a white beard, with a red cloak tucked up round his knees; but I have never been afraid to do something a little out of the ordinary, I think I may claim, particularly if it is to save kiddies from disappointment.

The journey, as a matter of fact, was uneventful (though I

thought I heard some silly giggling as I turned into Dyson Road), and I reached the Vicarage without accident. The front of the house was ablaze with lights, but the lane itself was very dark, which made it a matter of some difficulty to find the side gate. Still, it was not many minutes before I was safely inside the garden and, leaving my bicycle by the hedge, began to make my way cautiously up a narrow gravel path.

It would have been a kindness had Mrs Somers thought of posting somebody with a light to guide me in, and I can only suppose that her anxiety not in any way to disappoint the children led her to neglect this small attention. The result was that I must have branched off the direct route to the house and, after fruitless knocking, entered a greenhouse, which I naturally took to be the conservatory. I suppose I must have taken half a dozen steps before the strong smell of damp earth, the heat of the place (excessive for December), and the complete absence of light combined to make me realize my mistake. I immediately turned round, though not apparently through a hundred and eighty degrees, and stepped into a cactus – an awkward enough customer even for an unbearded man. This mishap made me, I am ashamed to say, momentarily lose my composure, and in wrenching myself free I incautiously stepped backwards off the duck-boards, lost my balance and toppled, rather than fell, into a trough or container of some soft flour-like substance, which the vicar told me later was horticultural soot.

Like most men who have led a busy active life I have once or twice before found myself at a loss in dark confined spaces, and experience has taught me the vital importance of standing absolutely still. Not indefinitely of course, but long enough to allow the mind to formulate a plan of campaign. On this occasion I adopted the same course, and very soon decided that I had only to regain the duck-boards and, keeping my left foot in contact with their edge, follow them to the door. Sure enough, some half-dozen paces brought me to the end, and extending my right hand I was greatly relieved to find it in contact with what must be the handle of the door. To this I gave a half-turn, and was at once aware of a fine but persistent jet or spray of water which seemed to come at me from every direction. The explanation, that I ought of course to have kept my *right* foot in contact with the duck-boards, did not immediately occur to me, and I fear that I did some little damage in my anxiety to be gone, before I understood that I was now at the wrong end of the greenhouse. Thinking back over the incident I am inclined to agree that my wisest step, after that first instinctive leap backwards, would have been to search again for the controlling handle or tap and turn the water off. But men do not always, in emergency, do the wisest thing. What I very much resent is the suggestion that I at any time panicked or lost my head. The simple fact that, when on my way back down the greenhouse, I kept the soot-trough constantly in mind and on this occasion disentangled myself from the cactus with proper deliberation should be enough to scotch *that* snake.

That I was vexed and put out by the whole business I do not deny. Indeed, when I regained the dry open air my intention was to return straight home, however bitter the disappointment might be to the kiddies, and it was pure chance that led my footsteps to the conservatory instead of to my bicycle. Having got so far, however, I thought it my duty to let some member of the household know that I was unfortunately unable to give away the presents as arranged. Accordingly I made my way through the back portions of the house, where I saw nobody except a woman working at a sink, who gave a shrill cry as soon as I accosted her and locked herself into a cupboard. I have no patience at all with female hysterics and simply passed on into the hall, which was brightly lit and gaily decorated with streamers and balloons. From a closed door leading, as I knew, into the dining-room came the sound of youthful voices and the clatter of tea-cups, but the hall itself was empty, and it was while pondering what best to do that I happened to catch sight of my reflection in a large and, to my mind, rather rococo looking-glass.

I at once decided that my best plan, after all, would be to go quietly home and telephone from there. One is prepared, of course, to look odd, even ridiculous, in the garb of Father

Christmas, but I was certainly not prepared to present myself in company in the state to which I was now, through no fault of my own, reduced. The gown itself was not seriously torn, except about the hem, but my face was so mottled and streaked with soot and perspiration that I do not believe even my old colleagues would have recognized me. Rivulets of blackened water had run down the full length of my beard, which was sadly awry. My hands, naturally enough, were coated with soot and dried blood (a good mixture I remember thinking – so oddly does the mind associate in times of stress – for brussels sprouts). There was leaf-mould not only on my boots but even on my scarlet hood, and twined about my right sleeve was some kind of creeper with curious fleshy leaves.

It was in trying, with an understandable gust of annoyance, to shake or flick this last encumbrance from me that my right-hand came by ill-luck into contact with an old-fashioned gong immediately behind me. A low resonant boom rang through the house, and I had scarcely time to take one quick step towards the front door when the dining-room door was thrown open and Somers himself stood framed in the aperture.

'St Chrysostom!' he said.

My first concern was to assure him that the sounding of the gong had been purely accidental. One does not, naturally, summon people intentionally in such a way – least of all in their own homes.

'I was flicking off a creeper – ' I began.

'Flicking off a creeper!' he repeated, in the voice of a man who attaches little or no meaning to what he is saying. 'My dear fel – Not you, Jackie. Get back, boy, and shut the door.'

He was too late, however. A little red-haired boy, who belongs I think to the butcher, peered round his legs and set up a cry of 'He's come! He's here! Father Christmas is come down the chimley!' At once there was a rush from within the room, and a cluster of boys and girls pushed and jostled their way into the doorway. I realized that it would never do, whatever my personal vexation, to forget the part I was supposed to be playing. Accordingly, I did my best to smile cheerily at

ie youngsters, and gave them a welcoming wave of one of my
lackened and bleeding hands. 'Merry Christmas!' I said.

One or two of the smaller ones started to cry, but I very soon
ut an end to that.

'Stop that noise this instant!' I ordered, and there was an
nmediate silence. I have not been a schoolmaster for thirty-
ve years for nothing – little though it was that I got, in
nother sense, I am bound to say.

Mrs Somers had by this time worked her way to the front of
he group, and I heard the vicar tell her, still in the same low
emused voice 'All he *says* is that he was flicking off a creeper.'
t was a difficult situation for her, in some ways, as for me. But
he is a well-bred woman, and her years of training as a hostess
old her instinctively what to do.

'Perhaps, dear,' she said briskly, 'Father Christmas would
ike a wash.'

'Of course, of course,' the vicar said, coming forward while
is lady began to shepherd her charges back into the dining-
oom.

'What on earth, Wentworth?' he went on, when the door
was safely shut. 'My dear fellow, you are all wet, apart from
the – Where have you *been*?'

'I have been in your greenhouse,' I said shortly.

'In my green – ? To shelter from the rain? I had no idea –'

'Not to shelter,' I said, and there was something in my voice
that warned him, I think, that I did not wish to pursue the
matter at present.

'Come along, anyhow,' he cried. 'Come along and wash.
This way, this way. Mind the gong.'

'I am neither blind nor incapable, thank you,' I said irrit-
ably. 'It was by pure mischance that I had my back turned
when shaking or flicking –'

'Shaking or flicking?' he said. 'Dear me! I hardly know –'
He has a tiresome habit of rushing into speech before one has
fairly begun what one has to say. 'By the *way*,' he added,
halting suddenly in front of a door, 'I suppose when you had –
er finished in the greenhouse, you remembered to shut the
door?'

'I doubt very much,' I replied, 'whether it makes any diffe
ence now whether the door is shut or open.' I did not, to te
the truth, very much care.

'My calceolarias!' he cried – or some such ridiculous expl
tive. 'In that case – in here, please. Forgive me!' And he w
off, leaving me to tidy up as best I might in peace.

Well, it had been an unlucky business in many ways. B
misfortunes, as I have said, can sometimes be turned to goc
account. The children were not at all frightened when I final
entered the room carrying a laden sack. Indeed they clustere
about me, demanding to know what it was like coming dow
a chimney; which one I had chosen; where my reindeer wer
and suchlike childish questions. 'You really made the tiny on
believe in Father Christmas again,' Mrs Somers told me late
on. 'You see, they had got rather too used to poor ol
Witherby. I do think it was clever of you to think of the soot.'

'Yes, yes. Yes, indeed,' Somers said. 'Though I could wish –
if you had thought of asking – however, there it is.'

I thought it best to leave it at that for the time being. Every
body was most kind, and even when I gave little Felicit
Bennings a pat on the head and a quantity of soot, which mus
have somehow lodged in my sleeve, fell on her flaxen curls, th
incident passed off with general good humour. There wer
games and crackers, and really, despite my damp gown, th
years seemed to roll away. It was quite a disappointment whe
people began to leave. I was playing 'Puss in the Corner' – a
my age! – when Mrs Somers came running from the telephon
to say that I was wanted at once at the Parish Hall.

'It's Miss Stephens,' she said. 'She says the curtain goes up
in ten minutes, and where on earth have you got to?'

'God bless my soul!' I cried. 'The play! I had forgotten al
about it.'

The Play

I hardly know how the play happened to escape my memory, except, of course, that I was late at the Vicarage on account of the imbroglio in the greenhouse and one thing and another. Goodness knows it has been in my mind often enough the last few weeks, with rehearsals three days a week, and now one of my two arm-chairs borrowed for scenery. I am to be Alfred Lockhart, who comes in first and says 'Oh – I say, is this right?' not the Professor. Lockhart is described in the directions – the play we are doing is, of course, *The Linden Tree*, by a man called Priestley, about whom I know little though I remember once reading what seemed to me a very much too highly-coloured account of life in a preparatory school by a man of the same name – at any rate Lockhart is described as 'a precise, anxious, clerkly, middle-aged man', which made me chuckle when I read it. 'Hardly the part for me, Miss Stephens,' I pointed out; but she said she was sure I could do it very nicely. I suppose that is the point of acting, in a way. To be somebody different, I mean. If we all went on the stage to play ourselves it would be just like everyday life, which nobody wants to pay half a crown to see, I take it, or even a shilling farther back.

I dare say Sidney Megrim has had a lot of experience in producing, as we call it, but his manner is sometimes a little, well, abrupt, considering the difference in our ages. It is not after all as if one were being *paid* to make onself out to be 'precise and anxious' and all the rest of it – as is the case, for instance, when a younger Headmaster (*mutatis mutandis*, naturally) takes advantage of his position to administer a rebuff. At the very first reading of the play I had no sooner

said this opening line about 'Oh, I say, is this all right?' (W
were not in costume then, of course – strictly speaking: thoug
as a matter of fact I wear an ordinary suit when we are – b
even so I held up both hands as I spoke, to show surprise a1
doubt) – I had no sooner spoken than Megrim interrupt
with a quite gratuitous 'No, it is *not* all right, Wentworth. I
terrible.'

'Indeed?' I said. 'And in what precise manner – '

'Look,' he said. 'You have just been shown into the roo
by Mrs Cotton here – '

'By Miss Stephens,' I corrected.

'By Miss Stephens, if you prefer it, who is taking the part
Mrs Cotton, woman-of-all-work to the Linden househol
Right? You have come to see Mrs Linden. You expecte
therefore to be shown into the drawing-room. You find you
self in Professor Linden's study. Right? What's the good
gabbling off your opening line and *then* looking surprised
Come in. Look round the room. Register surprise – "Oh!" –
and off you go.'

'You mean exit?' I asked. 'At once?'

'Off you go with your speech, man. Now try it again, there
a good chap.'

I said nothing, but at once, as a good trouper should, di
my best to follow his instructions by looking round the roo
– St Mark's Hall, of course, actually – with growing astonish
ment.

'Get on with it, man!' Megrim said. 'You haven't come t
take an inventory of the furniture.'

It is almost impossible to get the feel of a part if one is to b
constantly interrupted.

'I have been shown in a good many wrong rooms in m
time, young man,' I began –

'I dare say,' he said. 'But not into this one. Again, please.'

I kept my temper, of course. As Miss Stephens said later, i
is all part of the game. 'You did it splendidly, Mr Wentworth
she told me. 'Sidney only makes us go through it over and ove
again because it helps to fix the lines in one's memory.'

'I see,' I said. 'Yes. I hadn't thought of that.'

When the telephone call came through to the Vicarage to that the play was due to begin in a few minutes it was a siderable shock to me. I am a firm believer in punctuality, l of course it is most important that all the actors should be sent on the opening night of a new play. New to Fenport, t is; the play has already, I understand, been performed where. But by a stroke of luck a Mrs Downing offered me ft in her motor to the Parish Hall, and I climbed in, still in Santa Claus outfit in which I had been helping to entertain children. There would be time enough to change when I to the Hall. At least, not time enough exactly, but one ows what one means. The important thing was to get there hout delay, and I am afraid I cried out a little impatiently en one of Mrs Downing's youngsters went back into the use for a missing balloon. 'It was a *red* one' the boy kept ing, as if that mattered. Children have very little sense of portion at times.

Megrim was standing at the back, or I suppose I should say ge' door, and addressed me at once, characteristically with-t bothering to say good evening.

'My God!' he said. 'Where have you *been*? We've had to g up.'

'I know that,' I replied, overlooking the blasphemy. 'I was the Vicarage when the call came. I am sorry, but – '

'The curtain, man, the curtain!' he cried. 'Muriel Stephens n now, dusting round and gagging. They got impatient. Get as quick as you can and never mind the make-up.'

'At once!' I cried, and ran past him through the dressing-m.

I cannot think how I came to forget that I was still wearing absurd red gown and rather soot-stained beard in which I d passed the earlier part of the evening. Looking back on it, uppose the rush, and my anxiety not to keep Miss Stephens d the audience waiting, momentarily disturbed my judge-nt. One must remember, too, that I was already 'in costume' d so not unnaturally felt ready to 'go on'. Even a more perienced actor, I dare say, might become confused if he had rush at a moment's notice from one engagement to another.

I do not acquit myself entirely from blame, but as a f
minded man I consider it was part of Megrim's duty, as p
ducer, to say a word of warning about my clothing. Be tha
it may, I lost no time in making my entry and, after adjus
my eyes to the glare of the footlights and taking a quick l
round the stage, as instructed at rehearsal, repeated
opening line.

'Oh, I say,' I said, 'is this right?'

Of course, strictly, I should have been shown in by M
Stephens, or 'Mrs Cotton' to give her her stage name, bu
she was already there, dusting and so on, that could not
helped. In any case as it turned out, it did not matter. M
Stephens turned round, duster in hand, and instead of reply
with *her* opening speech (which runs, as a matter of f:
'Right? It's as right as we can make it. Nothing's right n
nor ever will be, if you ask me,' and so can hardly be descri
as difficult to memorize), simply stood and gaped. No do
she was surprised by my appearance, but as an actress
considerable experience – however, there it was. The audie
had broken into loud laughter immediately on my openi
line, so it may be that, even if she had taken her cue, she wo
not have been heard.

The situation was a difficult one for both of us. The laugh
grew in volume and I felt completely bewildered. I am
stranger to merriment, for a schoolmaster's life is by no mea
the dull and colourless affair that some people make it out
be, nor am I without the means of quelling it when it threate
to grow beyond bounds. But on this occasion I felt quite a
loss – until happening to put my hand up to my chin, as is n
habit when puzzled or upset, I encountered my beard and
once became aware how incongruous my costume must appe
in a modern play, even at Christmas time. It was difficult
know what to do for the best. Somebody off-stage was shouti
'Come off the stage, you fool!' which did not help. But wh
particularly distressed me was to catch sight of Mrs Wheel
a lady whom I respect and admire, sitting in the front row ar
looking over her handkerchief at me with eyes that, unless

m much mistaken, were filled with tears. To her, at least, I felt
hat some explanation was due.

'I was unfortunately delayed, Mrs Wheeler,' I began, step-
ing forward to the footlights. 'There was a slight imbroglio in
he Vicarage greenhouse – '

I got no further, partly because I saw that Mrs Wheeler was
doubled up as though in pain, and partly because at this point
omebody, Megrim I suppose, pulled the curtains across and I
had much ado to avoid becoming seriously entangled in the
olds. So that was that.

We rang up again, as the saying goes, about ten minutes
ater, after Megrim had made a short speech to fill in the time
while I was busy changing and making up. It all went off very
well, I think. It was a little awkward, naturally, to have to
epeat my opening line, with which the audience were by now
amiliar, but I carried it off by varying the intonation.

'Oh, I *say*!' I said. 'Is *this* right?'

'Well, it's better,' some fool at the back called out (I suspect
Willis), and there was renewed laughter; but neither Miss
Stephens nor I took any notice, and after waiting for the noise
to subside, went quietly on with the play. I must say, everybody
seemed to enjoy it. I make no claim to be an actor, but I confess
there were tears in my own eyes during my final scene with
Professor Linden (actually Major Thorpe, from West Acre),
when we discuss the need for colour and vision in education.
How true that is! Major Thorpe I thought excellent. So indeed
were all the others, and it was a real surprise to me at the end
to hear my own name called out first of all. The proper thing,
of course, as the author was not present, would have been to
call upon the Major, or possibly the producer, to take a bow. I
took no notice therefore, affecting not to hear; but the shout
was taken up in all parts of the hall, and the clamour eventually reached such proportions that I was reluctantly forced to
step forward and raise a hand to stop it.

'Ladies and gentlemen,' I said, when I was able to make
myself heard, 'I am at a loss to know why I am singled out in
this way. This is my first appearance on any stage – or rather,'

I added with a smile, 'in a sense my second, as a gentleman a the back has just reminded me. I hope it will not be my last.'

'So do we,' cried Miss Stephens: a remark which was greete with such prolonged and good-humoured applause that found it by no means easy, hardened as I am to such scenes b innumerable Prize-givings and so on, to restrain my emotion.

'It has been a great privilege,' I continued, 'to learn some o the elements of this great art in the company of so gifted an distinguished a – er – cast. To Miss Stephens, who first enliste my aid in this enterprise; to our indefatigable producer, M Sidney Megrim; to Major Thorpe, for whose performanc tonight I feel sure the knowledgeable and incisive dramati critic of the *Advertiser* will find the right word, if right wor there be; to Miss Edge, but for whose painstaking make-up –

I had intended to conclude the list of those who had helpe in one way or another with the production by adding 'to al these I owe a debt that I can never hope to repay,' or som such suitable, and indeed sincere, phrase. But the applause anc clapping that followed each name as I mentioned it was s enthusiastic that I fear I lost the thread of my own remarks Indeed, during the particularly prolonged (and I am sure well-deserved) burst of cheering occasioned by my reference to Mis Edge, our make-up artist, my mind unaccountably wandere to the earlier part of the evening and I was unable to restrair an involuntary exclamation of dismay.

'God bless my soul!' I cried. 'I left my bicycle at the Vicarage.'

There was so much laughter at this – in which, after a momentary bewilderment, I readily joined – that I thought it best to leave the matter where it rested and give way to Megrim, who took the opportunity to say a few words of thanks on his own behalf.

So ended a memorable evening. Everybody has been more than kind, especially to one who took, after all, only a comparatively minor part. Even Odding, a man whom I have perhaps judged too hastily, came up to tell me that I had given him the best evening of his life. I am too old a hand to take such exaggerated praise at more than its face value. Still, there

no denying that kindness, as one gets on in life, is very
rming.

One has much to be thankful for. It has been a tiring day,
t without moments of difficulty that might easily, but for a
tain – 'knack', shall I call it? – that only years and experi-
ce can bestow, have ended in disaster. But the ending has
en a happy one. I feel that I am beginning to take a full part,
ewarding part, in the life of the village that is now my home.
ae does not want to become sentimental, but I think I may
iim that I am 'accepted' in Fenport, that I belong. And that,
an old man who has sometimes been lonely, means much.

My mind is at rest, what is more, about my bicycle. The
ar rang up to say that he had stumbled across it by his
rden gate and had put it in the greenhouse for the night. So
s, in his own rather odd phrase 'more or less under cover'.

A Disappointing Start

It is not easy for a retired schoolmaster to live in the manner
which he is accustomed (and *that* is no great shakes, in
conscience) on a small pension and the few shillings saved fro
a lifetime spent trying to knock the elementary principles
mathematics into a succession of thick-headed Burgrove bo
One does not expect, naturally, to be able to afford televisi
sets and all the other fal-lals that I am told are now necessiti
– necessities, forsooth ! – for millions of people who have nev
heard of Pythagoras and could not solve a second-degree equ
tion to save their lives, but a man likes a pipe of tobacco no
and again, and really there are times when one hardly kno
where to turn with collar-attached shirts coming back in
parlous condition from the laundry at one-and-fourpence
time and baked beans, which I do *not* like, almost a luxu
now. Something ought to be done, though it is hard to sa
what. I certainly have no intention of accepting charity, fro
the Government or anyone else, at my time of life. Not that
would have accepted it as a young man, I need hardly say.

All that, however, is beside the point. I am not in my dotag
yet by any manner of means, and prefer to plough my ow
furrow so long as I have my health and strength. My hearin
is remarkably good, considering, and as to my eyesight no
much escapes me, as Mrs Bretton found to her cost only th
other day when she forgot to dust behind the clock. At th
same time I do not altogether care for the idea of taking som
fiddling coaching or tutoring job down here in Fenport, wher
I have other interests and, perhaps I may say without im

modesty, a certain standing. The answer for a man in my position seems to me to be some form of part-time occupation elsewhere, it might be as companion or adviser to some young man or family, just for two or three months in the year. I fancy, with my experience, I could be of some assistance in any one of a number of situations that come to mind – and I use the word 'situation' in its widest sense, of course. One has not held the post of Headmaster's right-hand man (which I think I may say I was in my later years at Burgrove, despite young Rawlinson's tendency at times to – well, push himself forward a little more than his qualifications or attainments warranted) without acquiring the administrative ability and, shall we say, *savoir faire* that could be of inestimable value in, for instance, arranging a tour abroad, buying tickets and so on, or in taking charge of whatever it might be while others were temporarily absent. That kind of thing. Difficulties constantly arise, as I well know, where there is need for someone absolutely trustworthy to take over until matters sort themselves out. At any rate, we shall see.

Retired schoolmaster, B.A. (Oxon) wd consider short-term employment, up to 3 mths if interesting work. Posns of trust, organization, etc. Willing to travel, within limits. Accustomed sole charge individuals or gps. No agencies or divorce work.

I should not myself have thought it necessary to make the final provision, particularly in an advertisement for insertion in *The Times*, but an old friend whom I consulted on this matter tells me that it is advisable, if one wishes to avoid unpleasant entanglements. I am not exactly certain what 'No agencies' means, as a matter of fact, but I can well believe that it is something I should not care to be mixed up in. One hears of detective agencies, for instance. I can put my finger on the guilty party as promptly as any man when it is a matter of paper-dart-throwing or that bizarre business of Matron's overshoes, and I dare say the knowledge of human nature one acquires as a schoolmaster would stand me in good stead if I were ever called upon to investigate more serious crimes. I had

no doubt whatever in my own mind about the theft of Mi
Stevens's ducks down here the other week. Foxes, indeed
'That was a two-legged fox, if ever I saw one,' I told her, an
would very soon have named the culprit had she not alread
been paid compensation by the Hunt secretary. Still, that wa
all in the way of friendship. It is a very different matter t
stand about in shrubberies at so much the hour and jot dow
the numbers of young men who arrive in Jaguars. The num
bers of their cars, that is to say. I shall certainly decline an
offers of work of that kind.

One will have to feel one's way. Who knows? Perhaps b
this time next week I shall be far away from my little cottag
in Fenport, engaged in some employment of a confidentia
nature. The years seem to roll away. One is on the threshol
of, if not adventure at least a change. That is the great thing
I might almost be a young man again, eagerly awaiting th
start of my first term as an assistant master. We shall see, as
have already said.

There have been no replies as yet to my advertisement, apar
from a suggestion that I might be interested in investing £200
in a second-hand furniture shop shortly about to open in South
Wales. I am not. I have not put aside fifty pounds a year from
my earnings ever since I was twenty-five in order to provide
Welshmen with dressers and mahogany chests-of-drawers
Other considerations apart, I know nothing about second-
hand furniture shops except that I have yet to see a customer
enter one. I remember, years ago, asking a colleague why it
was that such shops always kept half their furniture outside on
the pavement, but he did not know. He said it was the same
with people who sold ladders and enamelled baths. 'But not
butchers or chemists,' I objected, and he agreed. One would
have thought there would be by-laws.

My copy of *The Burgrovian* arrived by the same post as this
extraordinary suggestion and I was skimming through 'Notes
and News' (young Phillips has been playing hockey for Sand-
hurst, I see, though they have got his second initial wrong

ain) when an odd thought made me smile. 'Mr A. J. Wentworth's many friends, past and present, will be interested to ar that he has gone into the second-hand furniture business' what a scoop that would be for next term's issue! But it is t my duty, I am thankful to say, to provide sensational items my old school magazine. The whole thing is not worth a oment's thought.

Megrim came in about the Debating Society, and I asked n (quite casually, of course, and without giving anything vay) if he happened to know anything about second-hand rniture in Wales.

'You ask the most extraordinary questions, Wentworth,' he id. 'I imagine it is like second-hand furniture anywhere else. uge wall mirrors and purplish bureaux with dangling brass ndles. Why?'

'Oh, nothing,' I said. 'It doesn't matter.' I then tried to ange the subject, but Megrim is one of those people who orry at a casual conversation like a dog with a bone.

'Suppose I were to ask you whether you knew anything out ironmongery in Northumberland,' he said. 'Wouldn't at seem to you a bit odd? Or no, as a matter of fact I suppose wouldn't. *Do* you know anything about ironmongery in orthumberland, Wentworth?'

I told him, as far as I remember, that I knew nothing about onmongery, or about Northumberland either for that matter. said, quite politely, that I was not in the least interested in onmongery and that, if everything was now settled about the ebate, I had some rather important letters to write. But you ight as well give a hint to a rhinoceros.

'*I'm* not interested in second-hand furniture,' he said, with look round my room which I very much resented, 'unless it's od, that is. But I *am* interested, naturally, in why you should interested. In South Wales of all places. Of course, if it's a cret —'

'There is nothing secret about it,' I interrupted, well know-g what would happen in a place like this if anybody thought ere was. 'It simply happens — a friend of mine was asking me out it. I am only sorry I bothered you with the thing.' I do

not care for prevarication, but with a certain type of persist
bore one sometimes has no alternative.

'I see,' he said. 'I tell you what though. You know Robe
up the lane?'

'Well?' I said.

'Well, I've got an idea he, or it may have been his sister, us
to be in Antiques or something more or less in those parts.]
might be able to help. I'll send the old boy along to you, sh
I?'

'It is very kind of you,' I began, 'but – '

'No trouble,' he said in that off-hand way of his. 'I'm goi
that way in any case.' And he took himself off before I had
chance to tell him for goodness' sake to mind his own busine
If only I knew of an ironmonger from Westmorland or soɪ
such place to plague Megrim with I could soon put a stop ɪ
this nonsense.

Roberts came to the back door after tea to tell me he h:
something in the handcart outside I might care to look at.]
can't say I was greatly surprised, for these people always see
to get hold of the wrong end of the stick. Rather than invol·
myself in a long explanation to the effect that I was n
interested in buying furniture but in the second-hand furnitu
business (which I certainly am *not*), I accompanied Roberts ·
the gate in no very good temper.

'That's a Swansea piece, that is,' he said. 'As you'll like ɪ
know.'

It was a small chest of drawers, hardly fit even for a boy
dormitory, and quite useless to me. However, I offered the ma
half a crown to be rid of him. It did not seem fair that h
should have had his journey for nothing, under a misappre
hension that was probably not altogether his fault. But he wa
by no means grateful. He said it was a genuine antique. 'Wh
it's worth more than that as firewood,' he told me.

'I dare say,' I said. 'But there's the labour of chopping it up

In the end, feeling a little ashamed of having allowed i
temper to rule my tongue, I gave him ten shillings for it, whicl

can ill afford, and asked him to put the chest in the tool-shed. It seems a poor return, so far, for my advertisement in *The Times*.

Perhaps tomorrow's post will bring me something a little more promising.

A Missed Opportunity

It is all very well to say that all experience is an arch, a
Tennyson somewhere or other claims, wherethro' gleams tha
untravelled world and so on and so forth. I used often to recit
the passage, I remember, in my younger days when things wen
a little awry – to myself, that is: one does not declaim poetr
aloud up and down the corridors of a first-class preparator
school! – and was much comforted by it at times. We live an
learn, I suppose, would be another way of saying the sam
thing. But I very much doubt whether Alfred Tennyson, with
all respect to his memory, ever had such a day as I have had
with nothing to show for it but a torn trouser-leg and a pocke
full of unwanted oats. All experience indeed! A hundred and
fifty miles all told, and an umbrella riddled with small sho
through no fault of my own, at the end of it. What kind o
untravelled world gleams through *that* particular arch, one i
tempted to ask.

Whatever it may be, I feel disinclined this evening, with
what I fear may be a heavy cold coming on, to explore it. One
begins very seriously to doubt whether the insertion of my
advertisement in *The Times*, asking for short-term work in
positions of trust, etc., was altogether wise. Quite apart from
being pestered with second-hand furniture down here in Fenport, some of the offers of employment made to me through
the post have been ridiculous. One does not become a Bachelor
of Arts, I should hope, in order to exercise dogs from 2.30 to
4.0 p.m. every afternoon except Thursdays. Nor am I the man,
as those who know me best will agree, to recommend hosiery

total strangers on a commission basis! There are times when
ally think the world has gone mad.

Still, to be fair, as I always try to be, the post in search of
ich I set off to Wiltshire early this morning appeared to be
y much more in my line of country and might indeed have
ted me well, but for a chain of ill-luck such as I have rarely
perienced. An opening as companion-secretary to a gentle-
n temporarily incapacitated by an accident while hunting
he kind of thing I am looking for, at twelve guineas a week
h board and keep and travelling expenses refunded after
interview if unsuccessful. I had little doubt in my mind, as
walked to the station to catch the 8.45 local to Southampton,
t provided this Colonel Ripley proved to be of a congenial
st of mind we should very soon come to terms. Nor have I
y reason to doubt *now* that we should have done so, had 1
n permitted to meet the gentleman.

Little is to be gained by jotting down the details of this
xatious business. The milk has been spilt, in every sense of
e phrase, and there is an end of it. But I owe it to myself to
int out that had adequate transport been available at Stens-
ll nothing of the kind would have arisen. I was thunderstruck
en a rather dull-witted porter there told me that no buses
n past the Manor House on Wednesdays. 'There was a car
me to meet the 11.48 down from Blandford,' the man said.
ut I doubt it could have been for you, seeing you just got off
e 12.6 up from Temple Combe. Not that Mrs Ripley didn't
back empty in a bit of a taking, at that.'

There seemed no point in explaining to the fellow that I had
en badly advised by a ticket-inspector at Bournemouth
est, so I simply asked him what I had better do. After some
ought he told me in his slow country way that Grimley's van
uld be coming 'up street' in a minute or two and might be
le to drop me 'there or thereabouts', as he was pleased to put

Having no alternative I agreed to this curious approach to
future employer, and very soon found myself jolting along
a bucket seat beside a civil young man, who seemed
nuinely sorry that he had not the time to take me round past
e Manor gates. He was going 'sort of more along the back of

their place, like', he told me (How strangely these people ta
but would drop me at the nearest point, where I could
across a couple of fields and up through the farm. "
minutes,' he said, 'at the outside', and late though I wa
seemed the best thing to do. One cannot pick and cho
really, when nothing else offers.

I could not foresee, of course, that a heavy downpour of r
would catch me out in the open as soon as I had entered
second of the two fields indicated to me. Naturally I had
umbrella with me, but I most certainly did not wish to app
for my interview with sodden trouser legs and I theref
turned left-handed and made all possible haste along
hedgerow to a barn or shed which stood in the near corne
the field, intending to shelter there through the worst of it
was here that I had my first stroke of misfortune. The build
was very dark inside, and though I could just make out tha
contained some kind of machinery I had no warning that th
was need to exercise more than my usual caution until I h
pened, while shaking my umbrella, to engage the crook o
with what must I suppose have been a lever or handle. I ga
no more than a slight tug, to free it, and at once noticed
whirring and clanking noise suggesting that some sort
mechanical operation had been set in motion. Then a co
siderable quantity of oats, a very considerable quantity, v
precipitated over my head and shoulders from above.

This incident, though momentarily startling and confusi
in the indifferent light, was not in itself, to one who is acc
tomed to life's ups and downs, more than a passing inco
venience, and I should not have mentioned the mishap h
not its immediate consequences proved so vexatious. Oats a
less easy to brush off the clothing than some other kinds
cereal, and though I did my best in the few minutes th
elapsed before the rain stopped I suppose it was inevitable th
I should leave what amounted to be a trail behind me
resuming my walk. Be that as it may, I soon became aware th
I was being followed by several farmyard fowls, whi
appeared from nowhere after the manner of these creatur
Their number and speed increased rapidly, to my dismay,

at by the time I had reached the farther hedge, beyond
nich the roofs and chimneys of what must be Manor Farm
ere clearly visible, they had become a serious embarrassment.
am not easily put out, but no one cares to arrive for an
ppointment attended by a flock of gaping poultry. I therefore
ade an attempt to drive them off with gestures of my
nbrella, which I still think was the only sensible course in the
rcumstances. There was an outburst of cackling and one or
vo fowls rose into the air with the usual exaggerated loss of
athers, and I was preparing to take advantage of the diver-
on to slip through a gateway when I heard the sound of
nning feet and a man's voice from beyond the hedgerow
outing, 'Get over left there, quick!'

Not knowing to whom he was speaking I checked the swing
was taking at a particularly pertinacious hen (a White Wyan-
otte, I think) and unluckily lost my grasp on my umbrella,
hich flew into the hedge some distance to my right, where it
dged quivering. At once there was a further cry of 'There he
es!' followed by the roar of firearms, and I found myself
mporarily blinded by a mêlée of excited hens.

'Hi!' I called out. 'I say there!'

'What the devil are *you* doing?' a rough voice replied, and
oking up I saw a tallish man in gaiters at the gateway, with
younger fellow (looking pretty scared, I thought) behind him.

'I might well ask you that,' I answered, getting to my feet in
o very good temper. 'Is it your custom in this part of the
ountry to shoot at visitors without warning?'

'There was a fox,' the younger fellow said sheepishly. 'In
he hedge yonder. They get after the fowls, see?'

'Fox, indeed!' I said, and without another word I strolled
cross and retrieved my umbrella, which, to my great morti-
ication, I found to be shot through and through.

'You tailored un good and proper, Fred,' the tall man said
vith a laugh.

'Somebody will have to pay for this,' I remarked sternly. 'It
s a most outrageous thing.'

'You was trespassing,' the man said. 'Creeping about the
edges. Who are you, and what do you want?'

'See them birds pecking at his turn-ups?' the young hobbl
dehoy put in. 'He's mostly chock-a-block with grain, or som
thing of that, if you ask me.'

'So that's the game, eh?' the other man said.

'My name is Wentworth,' I told them, sick and tired of th
meaningless folly. 'I have an urgent appointment with Colon
Ripley. Be so good as to direct me to the Manor House at onc
please.'

My manner must have made it clear to them with who
they had to deal. But even so I was obliged to show these tw
fools my letter from the Colonel before they would permit m
to pass. 'Best call in at the farmhouse and see Mrs Jellaby,' th
elder said finally, perhaps in a belated attempt to mak
amends. 'She'll maybe run you up in the Land Rover.'

One would have thought that I had had enough trouble an
delay already, and might now hope that the final stages of th
tiresome journey would be comparatively plain sailing. But
have often found that if ill-luck dogs one at the start of a da
it is difficult to shake it off completely before evening. On
thing leads to another, as they say. Had I not been opening an
shutting my umbrella as I descended the steepish track into th
farmyard (in order, of course, to see whether the ribbing ha
been as irretrievably ruined as the fabric), I dare say I shoul
not have been attacked, or at least menaced, by what at fir
glance I took to be a bull. With the quick instinct of a countr
man I made a sideways leap on to a kind of trestle or stand fo
milk churns that chanced to be at the side of the track, no
knowing of course that it was in fact a wheeled trailer – sti
less that my weight would raise the shaft, or towing-bar, fron
the ground and set the contraption in motion.

Heigh-ho! It's a weary world at times. Tennyson and hi
precious arch keep recurring to my mind as I sit by my gas fir
and ponder on the tricks that fate can play. To the Greeks, o
course, it was overweening pride that led to man's misfortune
but nobody, I imagine, will accuse me of that. Still, one mus
not make too much of what was, after all, no more than
gentle spill. Had the trailer overturned in the steeper part o
the track there might have been a nasty accident, but luckily i

pt going until we were fairly down on the more level midden, ᴦen the towing-bar met some obstruction and I was cata- ᴧlted on to a heap of – well, straw, and so on. Two churns, ᴇ of which at least seemed to be practically empty, had ᴦeady fallen off, and I suppose it was the considerable clatter ᴇy made as they rolled away into a cart-shed that brought a ᴄther heavily-built woman in slippers to the farmhouse door. 'What's the idea of this, then?' she asked.

I was anxious, as may be imagined, to give a full explanation my unceremonious arrival, but whether it was the partial ᴇtting I had had while running for shelter earlier on, or ᴦether it was some effect of grain dust, akin to hay-fever, I ᴧs seized by a most uncharacteristic fit of sneezing, and for ᴦne little time remained sitting where I had fallen unable to y a coherent word.

'Such a racket!' the woman said. 'I'd have thought it was ᴇ Last Trump, if there'd been lightning with it.'

'Atishoo!' I said.

'I don't know, I'm sure,' she said, coming nearer. 'Look at ᴧur trousers!'

'Atchoo – atchoo – a-*tisho*!'

'Have you come far,' the woman asked curiously, 'just to ve that carry-on?'

I continued to sneeze for some time, while the woman made ᴐ offer to help, contenting herself with a series of wondering ᴄclamations and the absurd observation that it never rains but pours. But at last the paroxysm began to abate and I was ᴐle to speak, though not at first freely.

'My name,' I said, struggling to my feet, 'is Woo – dear me my name is *Atcher* . . .'

'Is that your umbrella and all?' the woman asked.

I think it was the state to which my faithful old brolly (a ᴦesent from my colleagues, as a matter of fact, on my fiftieth ᴦthday) – it was the sad condition of my old friend, when I ᴄovered it from beneath the trailer, that made it clear to me ᴦat I must abandon any idea of calling upon Colonel Ripley, ᴑr that day at least. I decided to cut my losses, and take

myself off with the least possible delay. I had had abo
enough, to tell the truth.

'Perhaps you will be good enough to give a message
Colonel Ripley?' I began briskly. 'As you can see – '

'How you ever come to be on that trailer,' the woman sai
' "Wagon Train" isn't in it.'

'Never mind that now,' I said. 'Please tell your master th
Mr Wentworth was unable to keep his appointment toda
owing to a combination of – a – , a – , – Confound it!'

'You'd better let it come,' she said.

' – owing to circumstances over which I had no control. Ju
tell him that, please. And that I – that Mr Woo – Woo – o
devil take it, Woorasher! Say I shall be writing,' I shout
angrily. 'And good day to you.'

'I'll tell him you called,' the woman cried after me, ar
burst into peal after peal of totally unnecessary laughter. The
has been a sorry decline in manners, I fear, even in the countr
side.

So there it is. I suppose I should write some sort of explan
tion to Colonel Ripley, asking for another appointment, but
don't seem to have the heart for it, just now.

A Comfortable Billet

It has turned out very well in the end, as is often the case if one keeps one's head and lets things take their course. Some men, I dare say, would have given up after the unlucky experience I had on my first attempt to keep an appointment at the Manor House, Stenshall, Wiltshire, but schoolmasters have to learn to take the rough with the smooth. A very courteous letter from Colonel Ripley, regretting any inconvenience to which I had been put and suggesting a date for a second visit, decided me to try again – and here, in short, I am, snugly housed in a bedroom twice the size of my little crib at Fenport, and nothing in the way of draughts to speak of considering the age of the house.

Needless to say, my second journey down here went off without a hitch. Mrs Ripley drove me from the station, pointing out this and that as we went along. She is a charming lady, and we very soon found out that she was at school with a Miss Soulby whose nephew was at Burgrove during my time there, though we could neither of us remember the boy's name. A strange coincidence, which helped, I think. She is the kind of person with whom one at once feels at ease.

So, in his rather more boisterous way, is the Colonel. He has broken a leg, poor fellow, and is obliged to spend the day on a couch in his study, but looks very fit and healthy none the less. I naturally attempted an apology for my failure to get farther than Manor Farm on the Wednesday, but he brushed it aside with great good humour.

'Never laughed so much in my life, when I heard,' he said, slapping his good knee. 'Hens flying all over the place, shouting

and shots in the five-acre, and then down the hill you come like
a bat out of hell, balancing on a two-wheeled trailer by God
if Mrs Jellaby is to be believed, with oats pouring out of you
ears and milk scattering this way and that like a Goddess o
Plenty in her chariot – if I could have been *there* dammit ! –
and then *blam* ! head-first into a heap of dung and a hundred
and fifty-six sneezes to round it off. What an entry ! "Mary,"
I said to my wife – didn't I, Mary ? – "we must see this joker
if it's the last thing we do," I said, "and get the real inside
story." Well, you know how it is. Mrs Jellaby seems to think
you did it on purpose.'

'I dare say Mr Wentworth didn't find the experience very
funny at the time, dear,' Mrs Ripley said in her gentle way
while I was considering how best to take this very exaggerated
account of an admittedly absurd contretemps.

'It was certainly an unconventional way to arrive,' I said at
last with a smile. 'But these things happen.' And I gave them
a short account of what really occurred, to which I must say
they both listened with a great deal of appreciation. But then
I have always had the knack of telling a story, even if it is, up
to a point, against myself.

'Lucky you didn't hurt yourself, my boy,' Colonel Ripley
said, when he had had his laugh out. 'You must bill me for
those trousers – and the umbrella, of course. We might have
it mounted and hung up in the hall with the stags' heads and
other trophies. What is it, by the way – an eight-pointer ?'

I could not help joining in the laughter at this ridiculous
notion, and capped the Colonel's fancy by suggesting that
perhaps a plaster cast could be made of my ruined trousers.
This sally had even Colonel Ripley beaten, and after a little
silence he said that perhaps he ought to come to the point and
explain what kind of help he was looking for during his en-
forced idleness. It would be mainly answering the telephone,
I gathered, and seeing to this and that, as his wife had to be
out in the car, on farming and village matters, a great deal of
the time. I replied that I should be happy to make myself
useful in any way that was within my powers, and after some
further conversation about detail, the thing was settled. They

ave me a satisfying lunch of steak-and-kidney-pudding, which I always enjoy, and I left, promising to return with my baggage on the Monday. 'Let us know if you think of taking the short cut across the fields,' the Colonel called after me, but not being able to think of a suitable reply, I contented myself with a wave of the hand. The joke, in any case, is beginning to wear a bit thin.

So here, as I say, I am, safely back again at the Manor, with two very full and interesting days' work behind me. The Colonel has wide interests and keeps me busy on errands of one kind and another. Some of them might be thought a bit, well, *infra dig* for a man in my position, but I am no believer in making a fuss, especially as Colonel Ripley always remembers to preface an unusual request with the words 'Be a good chap,' which keeps things on a proper footing. Or so it seems to me.

It is a varied life. This morning, for instance, there was an order for linseed cake to be hastened, a note to take to old Mrs Coombes at the cottage, and a parcel to be got off. Then I had to ring Rogers at the Bull and tell him it was off ('Never mind what,' the Colonel said, in answer to my natural inquiry. 'He'll know'), give a message to the Rector about the Boys' Club and ask Mrs Jellaby how Phoebe was doing. 'Oh, and while you're in the village,' he went on, while I scribbled my instructions down on the pad I have bought myself (quite the secretary, eh?), 'you might look Mathers up and ask him about the insurance on Felicity. I want to be sure she is adequately covered. And get me a P.O. for 18s. 6d., will you? There's money in the drawer there. My wife has to be over at Sturminster all day in the car, I'm afraid, but there's an old bike of mine in the garage. It's got a basket, so bring a few leeks from the farm – only don't bring 'em to me, as you did with that fish yesterday, take 'em straight in to cook. There's a good chap,' he added, as my eyebrows rose.

There was also a message about a sack of potatoes that Mrs Ripley would deliver tomorrow, but I did not quite get the name of the person to whom I was to give it. Colonel Ripley gets rather impatient if one asks him to repeat things – it is his leg, I dare say, that makes him a little brusque at times – and

in any case there was no need to bother him. The message was
certainly to one of the people I had to call upon on other
matters, so I had only to keep asking as I went along. That is
what we used to call 'using your initiative' in the Army, where
one soon learns to find things out for oneself. Colonel Ripley
rather reminds me of my old C.O. in a way; he has a trick of
taking it for granted that one knows what he is talking about,
which of course is not always the case at first when the subject
is an unfamiliar one such as Army Council Instructions or, as
in this instance, livestock and so on. Had he made it clear to me
that Felicity was a mare, which I could hardly be expected to
know, my interview with Mrs Mathers (to take a case in point)
would certainly have gone off a great deal more smoothly.

When a rather slatternly woman came to the door of No. 7
Cadnam Row, in answer to my knock, and told me that Mr
Mathers was out, I naturally assumed that I was speaking to
Mrs Mathers, as indeed I was. 'Was it something important?'
she asked me, and I thought there could be no harm in passing
on the gist of my message, particularly as I was under the
impression that it concerned her.

'It was only that Colonel Ripley wanted to know,' I began,
' – the question is whether you are adequately covered.'

The woman flushed up and immediately glanced down at
her attire, and following the direction of her eyes I realized
that, in that sense, she certainly was not. To get over what
might have been a momentary awkwardness, I decided to
change the subject and, averting my eyes, asked her casually
whether she was expecting a sack of potatoes.

'It's no business of yours what I'm expecting, nor when,' she
cried furiously, and to my utter astonishment slammed the
door in my face, giving me no chance at all to explain, as I was
anxious to do in my own good time, that my opening question
referred simply to insurance. These country people take a deal
of understanding. It was a relief to move on to the Rectory,
where I had a pleasant chat with the incumbent, a man of
my own kidney with whom there was no need to fear mis-
understandings or embarrassments. He told me much about
Stenshall and its good people, which will be a help to me

as I go to and fro, and in return I explained that I was acting as companion-secretary to Colonel Ripley, while he was laid up. 'Though I'm more of a glorified errand boy than a secretary, it seems,' I added, smiling to show that I did not really take my employment amiss.

'Well, it's something to be glorified,' he responded. 'I only live in hopes of attaining that status!' And on that friendly note we parted.

My final call was upon Mrs Jellaby, down at the Manor Farm, an encounter which, to tell the truth, I put off as long as I could.

'Well I never!' she cried, throwing up her hands in mock astonishment. 'If it isn't Mr Woo-Woo-Woorasher!'

I had half expected something of the kind, after my previous meeting with the lady, and deliberately ignored the impertinence. 'My name is Wentworth,' I said quietly. 'Am I right in thinking I am addressing Mrs Jellaby?'

'I can't forget it – ever,' she said. 'I was in the front, not to tell a lie, when the clatter starts up, and I said to myself "It's the atomic!" I said, "Or if it's not that," I said – '

'Mrs Jellaby! I have been asked by my employer, Colonel Ripley – '

'And sneeze!' the woman went on, wiping her eyes. 'Sitting there in the muck, kind of baffled, and not a word out of you but A-ratchoo till I thought to myself – '

'Mrs Jellaby!'

'But there! Come in do, Mr Wentworth,' Mrs Jellaby said, pulling herself together at last. 'I'm forgetting my manners. A glass of cider won't do either of us any harm.'

I was somewhat loth, as may be imagined, to accept hospitality after what had passed, but I had my mission to fulfil and took three glasses before I could get to the point. I must say that Mrs Jellaby proved, on better acquaintance, to be a very amiable woman and quite devoted to Mrs Ripley, as who is not? She is inclined to be a little voluble, perhaps, and utterly unable, like all these farming folk, to appreciate that what is clear to her may not be equally clear to an outsider.

'Phoebe?' she said at last, in answer to my repeated

inquiries. 'We're not happy about her at all, not really. She's still not letting it down, tell the Colonel.'

'Dear me!' I said. 'Yes. I see. Not letting what down exactly, Mrs Jellaby?'

'Why, her milk,' Mrs Jellaby said, staring at me as though I were out of my mind. 'Whatever else, Mr Wentworth?'

'Of course, of course,' I said. 'I hadn't realized – that is to say, what precisely do you think is the cause of this – of the failure? Just in case the Colonel wants to know, you know.'

'They say I'm an out-of-date old silly, Mr Wentworth,' Mrs Jellaby replied, leaning forward very earnestly with her hands on her knees, 'but it's *my* opinion she's got a cold in her bag.'

'I see,' I said, wondering what some of my old colleagues would have thought of this extraordinary conversation. 'Yes. No doubt. One can only hope, in that case, that, unlike another lady I could name, she is adequately covered!'

I had her there! It was *her* turn not to understand what *I* was talking about.

A Cricket Dinner

'Where's that ass, Wentworth?'

I could hardly believe my ears when I heard my employer refer to me in this offensive way, and I dare say he could tell by my manner, as with a quiet 'I am here, Colonel Ripley,' I stepped into the study and stood waiting with my pad at the ready, that I was not accustomed to such treatment.

'Oh, there you are!' he said lightly. 'You mustn't mind me, Wentworth. Mary will tell you I call all my friends asses.'

If he expected to mollify me by the insinuation that I was now more of a friend than an employee he only partially succeeded.

'That may be. They are in a position to return the compliment,' I said warmly. 'I, unfortunately, am not.'

'You manage to make your point very nicely, all the same,' he replied with a good-natured grin, and feeling that honours were even I let the matter drop, particularly as Mrs Ripley gave me a conspiratorial wink, as much as to say 'You put him in his place very adroitly there, Mr Wentworth.'

'What's this I hear about your asking Mrs Mathers if she was expecting a sack of potatoes, you old rascal,' the Colonel went on, bursting into a roar of laughter. 'If *you*'d had eight children in nine years, and another on the way, I dare say – '

'Good heavens!' I cried, flushing to the roots of my hair. 'So that was why – I had no idea.'

'It's all over the village,' Mrs Ripley said. 'And nobody enjoyed the story more than old Mathers.'

The subject hardly seemed a suitable one for mixed company, I must say. However, it was not I that had brought it up.

'What an unlucky thing!' I said, really distressed. 'I shall certainly do my best to explain and apologize, to Mrs Mathers.'

But to my surprise they both opposed this plan. 'You'd have to choose your words pretty carefully,' the Colonel pointed out; and with this, on reflection, I agreed.

It is difficult to avoid putting one's foot in it occasionally in these unfamiliar surroundings. Still, I am picking things up very quickly as I go along and in another week or so ought to be thoroughly *au fait* with farming affairs. By then, of course, my visit will be drawing to an end. The Colonel's leg is mending rapidly – 'I have you to thank for that, Wentworth,' he told me the other day. 'You are the best spur to recovery an invalid ever had' (a compliment that I greatly appreciated, as he is by no means over-ready with praise) – and as soon as he can get about my usefulness here will be over. I shall be sorry to go, in many ways, for they are friendly people hereabouts and I think I may claim to have made quite a hit with them. Everybody seems to know who one is, and so on, in a remarkably short space of time and to be anxious to stop for a chat. Only yesterday a total stranger hailed me to inquire whether my hay-fever was better, which I am sure was well meant, though I am not as it happens a sufferer.

As a matter of fact, it may well be convenient for me to leave in the fairly near future. Other things apart, I have had a belated reply to my advertisement in *The Times* from a Mr Bennett, of London, inquiring whether I might be free to accompany his two boys to Switzerland in about a fortnight's time. *In loco parentis*, I gather. One does not get away to the Continent very often on a pension like mine, and it seems too good an opportunity to miss, all being well. Still, all that is in the future. For the moment, there are things to be seen to in the outhouses! Upon my word, I sometimes wonder what the world is coming to. 'Be a good chap and nip out to the loft over the stables,' the Colonel began, so I knew there was something rather menial in the wind. How the boys at Burgrove would smile if they could see their old master checking over apples in a granary and putting the affected ones in a basket to take to Mrs Jellaby later – though what the good woman wants with rotten apples is more than I can say.

Tonight, apparently, I am to represent Colonel Ripley at the Annual Dinner of the Stenshall Cricket Club, of which he is President, so that one cannot complain of a lack of variety here. If it isn't one thing it's another, I said to Mrs Ripley in an unguarded moment, and she agreed. Her sympathy and understanding mean a great deal to me at times. She would have made an ideal headmaster's wife, had things turned out differently all round, with just the right manner towards parents, and it grieves me to see her carrying pig-meal about in an old pair of breeches. That is clumsily put, but the sentiment is sincere. 'Let *me*, Mrs Ripley,' I said to her on one occasion, and rather than hurt my feelings by refusing she handed over the bucket and thanked me very nicely. I think the unexpected attention touched her quite deeply, which explains why she went away without remembering to tell me where to take the pig-meal. There are no pigs here, as far as I know, so I had to get rid of it as best I could. The point is that her husband rather takes her for granted, in my opinion – not that it is any business of mine, of course.

Cricket holds the Empire together I told them, as one good fellow to another, and they liked it. Everybody sang afterwards, though I had had no warning, mind, not a word till it was too late and off I had to go. The Colonel knew. Ripley must have known what I had to do and I did it, no thanks to him. He never said. Anybody ought to, when people have to speak, but there it was.

'I am speaking on the President's behoof,' I said, which was true, despite the fact that I didn't know until I was told. What I mean is nobody told me before. 'Call upon Mr Wentworth to propose toast,' some fellow said, and there I was. I wouldn't have nine times out of ten. I said that, too, making no bones about it to clear the air. Nine times out of ten I wouldn't, I told them, but this is the tenth. 'Have some more cider,' they said, but I refused, unless that was later. I never drink more when I have to speak. Actually it was later I dare say because I didn't know I was going to before, as it turned out. I am scribbling on my bed while I remember, in case I forget what I was going to say. The Rector spoke, I remember that, and I spoke and another man spoke about a whip-round for bats ('In the belfry?' I said to my neighbour, but had to nudge him and repeat it, by which time the man – not this man, the other – was thanking the wives for helping with tea, so the point was lost). Where was I? For two pins I would go to bed, but my pyjama top is missing. Play the game I told them and everybody cheered. 'Stand up the man who shot my umbrella!' I said, mixing *seria cum joco*, and they cheered again. Nobody stood up so I sat down, having no more to say at present. It is a rule I always follow when speaking, but they all shouted, 'Go on, go on!' and somebody said, 'You have forgotten the toast, sir.'

'What toast is that?' I asked, not having been told properly before, and the Rector said it was the Club, which was a great honour for one who had so newly come among them. Not the Rector, naturally. I mean it was a great honour for me, or so I told them. 'I am only the Colonel's legate, of course,' I said – meaning to add 'his *broken* legate' for fun, but a bald-headed man got in first with the quip, and in the general laughter I could not think where in the world my pyjama coat can have got to. So I sat down again. Then the Rector proposed the toast of the Stenshall Cricket Club, and I made a short reply, which I forget. A Mr Binns told me I was the hit of the evening, but I ought to have been told before, in my opinion. Still, we all enjoyed myself and sang songs, which is the great thing.

It was under my shirt, of all places.

The days speed pleasantly by, with little of note to record. Colonel Ripley is up and hobbling about now, I am glad to say. Much of his old tetchiness has gone, too, which makes him easier to work with. Had he stepped into that puddle of pig-meal while he was still confined to his couch – not that he could have done so, naturally; I am merely drawing a comparison – he would have made a great deal more fuss about

, or I'm a Dutchman. Actually, it was a kind of mash for
chickens, which I should have disposed of elsewhere had I
known that my employer would be poking about in the shrub-
ery for some unexplained reason.

'Don't tell me *why* you put it there, Wentworth,' he said,
before I had so much as hinted that I had anything to do with
the matter. 'Some other time, perhaps, when I've an hour or
two to spare. We must just be thankful you didn't send it to
the Church Bazaar, along with that load of manure.' He was
smiling as he spoke, or I should certainly have resented this
unnecessary allusion to a perfectly understandable mistake. If
the Colonel has a fault, as he undoubtedly has, it is a tendency
to harp on trivialities that are over and done with. In any case
I am no stenographer, and errors are bound to occur occasionally when instructions are rattled off faster than I can write. It
was on the tip of my tongue to tell him that it was no part of a
companion-secretary's duties to dispatch manure, to the
Church Bazaar or anywhere else.

'Did I ever hear, by the way,' he went on, 'where my old
hats went to?'

They went to Lady Wimbury at the Grange, as he very
well knew, and as soon as she returned them with a short note
I realized that there had been a muddle and took immediate
steps to put things right. No harm whatever was done, as far as
I can see, except for a little staining outside the village hall,
which will wash off. It would have been different if the load
had been delivered *inside*.

'It would, yes,' Colonel Ripley agreed, when I pointed this
out. 'Now, be a good chap and give Mrs Ripley a hand in the
tables, will you?'

Be a good chap, indeed! Be a good ostler and general
factotum would be a likelier way of putting it.

Still, there are many compensations. I happened to be en-
joying the sunshine on the terrace after luncheon when two
or three shots rang out down by the farm. The men are
rabbiting, I expect.

'Hullo!' I heard the Colonel remark, through his open study
window. 'They're after Wentworth again!'

'Oh, I *hope* not,' Mrs Ripley replied, with her pleasa
laugh. 'He's such a dear, really.'

'I wouldn't have missed him for worlds,' the Colonel said.

I moved away then, of course, being no eavesdropper. Bu
had heard enough. The sun went in after a minute or two, b
I scarcely noticed it. There are things more warming th
sunshine.

In Foreign Parts

he snow-capped peaks tower upwards and the lake shimmers
the bright sunlight. Had I the pen of a Ruskin I dare say I
uld describe the scene with more vividness, though of course
ere is less need for that kind of thing now that so many
ople travel abroad. After all, when one has seen a thing for
eself one does not much want to hear what somebody else
ought about it – a point that modern writers often forget.
ne has one's snapshots, and so on, if memory proves
eacherous, whereas in Ruskin's time I suppose even picture
ostcards were something of a rarity.

Still, it is certainly very pretty here on Lake Lucerne – or
ierwaldstattersee, as it is rather cumbrously called on the map
ouristenkarte!) provided free by the hotel – and I cannot
elp congratulating myself on my wisdom in advertising for
mporary employment in *The Times*. There goes the steamer
r Vitznau, a typically foreign contraption, absurdly broad
the beam for such calm waters, though it all adds to the fun
a way. We shall be aboard her in a day or two, I expect,
hen the boys have had a proper rest after the long journey.
ake them about a bit and show them things,' Mr Bennett
id to me at our last interview, and I feel sure that a trip
und the lake would be in accordance with his wishes.
ucerne itself we must certainly see. Then there is the ascent
the Rigi, whence the views, so the hall porter tells me, are
ry fine. It will be best, I think, to draw up some kind of
ogramme after lunch.

We have already been up one mountain, as a matter of fact,
ther unexpectedly. Up to a point, that is. A man of my

experience does not take a couple of boys all the way up
mountain by accident, I need hardly say. What happened w
that on our way by train to Brunnen, where we are stayi₁
from Zurich whither we had flown by the night plane,
distinctly heard a woman say that this was a Schnellzug (s
was speaking in German, of course) and did not stop
Brunnen. As the train was then standing at Schwyz, which
luckily – or perhaps unluckily, as it turned out – knew to
the last stop before Brunnen, the last *station* that is to say,
bundled the boys out with our luggage in double-quick tin
only to find from a most helpful official that the train whi₁
had now left did in fact stop at Brunnen and that the next o₁
on would leave in an hour and a half. This was rather a face
as we had not yet breakfasted, but the official suggested th
we take a tram instead, from just outside the station, which ₁
very soon did. I thought it best not to explain our little slip-₁
to the boys, as William was getting fretful and even his eld
brother Geoffrey looked rather pale. Boys are happi₁
especially far from home, when they feel that everything
going smoothly, and a little harmless deception is oft₁
justified, in their own interests.

It was for this reason that, when the tram after a short r₁
reached the centre of Schwyz and everyone alighted, I co₁
cealed my annoyance at having been misdirected and, with
cheerful 'Only one more change now,' simply got out a₁
followed the rest into a waiting bus. Soon we were bowli₁
along a delightful valley and though, had I been in my ow
country and a little less tired, I suppose I should have ma₁
more careful inquiries, I had no hint of trouble until a co₁
ductor came along flourishing his clippers and I demand₁
'*Drei nach Brunnen*', with a wave of my hand at the two boy
The conductor shook his head and said 'Stoos', of which
could make neither head nor tail, so I simply handed hi₁
some money which unfortunately turned out to be Italia₁
How it came to be in my right-hand trouser pocket I cann₁
think. It is my custom when travelling abroad to make a ver
careful distribution of money, documents and other valuable
to ensure that each is handy as and when required. Thus o₁

present occasion I had our passports safely in my inside
ast pocket with the return air tickets pinned to the inner
k cover. Travellers' cheques, as always, were in my left-
ad hip pocket, which buttons, Swiss notes in my outside
ast pocket secured with a safety-pin, and so on. Any English
nge I tie up in a handkerchief as soon as the frontier is
ssed and keep for the time being in my left-hand trouser
ket. The small amount of Italian money I had brought with
in case we were able to make an excursion through the St
tthard tunnel should have been in my top right-hand waist-
t pocket, and I got the shock of my life when in trying to
lain all this to the conductor (with the aid of gestures, for he
ned a slow-witted sort of man) I put my fingers into the
ket in question and pulled out our return train tickets to
rich! These should by rights have been in the front fob
ket of my trousers, but I soon gave up the attempt to make
point clear to the conductor, for after a brief glance at
m he became so verbose and unintelligible that I had diffi-
ty in keeping calm. Geoffrey began to ask what was the
tter, and to gain time I blew my nose without proper fore-
ught and instantly scattered a considerable quantity of
all change about the bus.

verybody was most helpful in hunting about under the
ts, etc., for the coins, which to my astonishment proved to
Swiss.

Then where is my English money?' I cried involuntarily
oon as I saw that the money they were handing to me was
francs. This started a fresh search among a number of the
sengers who seemed to understand English, until I asked
m not to trouble. 'It will turn up, no doubt,' I said. 'I must
e put it somewhere else.'

Perhaps it's up the other nostril,' I heard young William
in a whisper to his brother, but I was unable to reprimand
at once for the impertinence as an English lady just in
nt of me was asking whether she could be of any help.

I thought I heard you asking for Brunnen,' she said. 'This
goes to Schattli, for the cable railway up to Stoos, you
w.'

'I see,' I said. 'Yes. And from there to Brunnen?'

'Well, you have to come back again to Schwyz, of co
and then there's a tram. But you might as well come righ
to Stoos while you are about it. It's lovely up there.'

So that is what we did. The boys seemed to think it
rather a long way round to Brunnen, but they enjoyed
cable railway and became much more lively when we fo
breakfast being served in a fine hotel up on the top. The l:
a Mrs Fitch who is staying at Brunnen apparently, was
kind, drawing our attention to Lake Lucerne away belov
our left and pointing out a number of the surrounding heig
She is a most friendly person, in the prime of life, and see
to be as relieved as I was when I finally found my English s:
change while taking my tobacco pouch from my right-h
hip-pocket. 'You shower money from *every* quarter, Mr W
worth,' she said gaily.

All that, however, is by the way. Here we are safely in
hotel, with the boys resting in their room on my instruct:
and I myself lazily watching the steamer grow smaller in
distance. It was a fortunate chance that Mr Bennett noti
my advertisement, and fortunate for me too that he had fo
himself unable, at the last moment, to accompany his two s
on their holiday abroad and so was obliged to look about f
trustworthy companion and squire for the lads. We very s
came to terms, and I must say that he has been most gener
in his provision for the jaunt. It is quite a new experience
me to have another man's money in my pockets to sp
(which reminds me that I really must get my small change :
so on re-sorted and properly disposed or goodness knows wh:
shall be finding in my waistcoat next. Piastres, eh? Or a ret
ticket to Baker Street!). But I dare say I shall quickly get u
to it.

Of course, it is a responsibility. But then, as I told
Bennett when he asked me whether I was used to taking cha
– this was at our first meeting, to be fair, before he had ha
chance to sum me up – I have taken parties of up to a do
boys abroad in my time and not a broken leg between the
He looked a little dubious at this recommendation fo

oment, but his brow cleared when I explained that I was
ferring to winter sports holidays. 'I see,' he said. 'Yes. I was
ot thinking of any physical danger so much. Geoffrey is a
eady, sensible boy as a rule, but William – the younger boy,
ou know – is apt to run a little wild at times. I suppose you – '
'Oh, that!' I said, laughing. 'You must set your mind at
est on *that* score.' It was really too funny to think that I might
e alarmed at the prospect of keeping two youngsters of eleven
nd thirteen in order. 'Why I have had fifteen of them at me
t once before now,' I began, recollecting an occasion at Bur-
rove when the electric light failed – but, realizing that he was
robably too busy a man to want to listen to stories of an
ssistant master's early days, I left it at that. In any case, by
he day after tomorrow at latest he should have my postcard
nnouncing our arrival after an uneventful journey, and his
ind will be at rest.

News of our little diversion up the Stooshorn has somehow
ot round the hotel, and there has been some flattering com-
ent on our energy in tackling a mountain before breakfast on
ur way out from England. 'Been up the Rigi yet, Mr Went-
orth?' somebody called out as we made our way in to lunch,
nd a party of young Dutchmen began to sing 'There'll always
e an England', *sotto voce*. I took it in good part, as one should
n a holiday, but when I pulled out my handkerchief during
he second course and some total strangers pretended to hunt
bout under their table I thought the joke had gone far enough
nd spoke pretty sharply to young William for giggling. It is the
rst time he has heard the rough side of my tongue, and I
hink it surprised him.

It looks as though somebody has been making a story out of
what was, after all, a very trivial mishap in the bus. I confess
hat I glanced momentarily at Mrs Fitch (who sits alone, I
otice), but meeting her wide-eyed and friendly smile dismissed
he thought as unworthy.

A Trip up the Rigi

I put on my pullover this morning, feeling in holiday moo
though one misses the extra pockets afforded by a waistcoa
and asked the boys at breakfast how they would like to mak
an expedition to the top of the Rigi, which seems to be th
thing to do here.

Geoffrey asked me how high it was, and I told him I believe
it was well over five thousand feet.

'Isn't that rather potty?' William said. He is at the ag
when they make rather a point of not being impressed an
has to be taken down a peg or two now and then, in a friendl
way.

'You must be careful not to trip over it when you aren
looking, William,' I said. 'That is, if you are thinking of mak
ing this trivial excursion on foot. Geoffrey and I are too old t
make light of five thousand feet and will be going up by train

'In a ship first,' Geoffrey said. 'In a jolly old *dampfschif*
Will Mrs Fitch be coming with us, Herr Wentworth?'

I suppose it is natural for boys to giggle at foreign words
though my own view is that that sort of thing should be kept fo
occasions when no foreigners are about whose feelings may b
hurt. I contented myself, for the moment, with a slight frow
to show that I was not greatly amused (often the best way witl
over-excited boys) and merely asked why he imagined that Mr
Fitch would be joining us.

'Well, she seems to. She came up the Urmiberg, I mean –
and that other place, when we went up by mistake.'

'The Urmiberg catches the worm,' William put in, and botl
boys laughed so immoderately at this senseless pun, if such i
could be called, that I was forced to check them. 'People are

>king round,' I said, and led the way out of the breakfast
>m (or *Speisesaal* in the local lingo), humming a little tune as
>ometimes do when a little put out. Not that William meant
>be impertinent, I think. Boys are apt to say the first thing
>t comes into their heads, whether it means anything or not.
It was pure chance, really, that Mrs Fitch happened to be
>the hotel entrance yesterday afternoon as we were setting
>t to walk to the cable-car that runs up to the Urmiberg from
>outskirts of Brunnen. Naturally she inquired where we
>re going, and one thing led to another as it so often does. She
>very well acquainted with the district and has already pro-
>sed to show us another little railway that starts quite near
>hotel and goes up to Morschach and Axenstein, whatever
>ey may be. If she had said Rosencrantz and Guildenstern it
>uld have been all the same to me. In any case, I see no harm
>it at my age. More was lost on Morschach's Fields, I fancy!
>t I must not let the sunshine and heady air of Switzerland
>tray me into young master William's habit of punning, how-
>er apt.

How astonishing, in passing, is the industry of the Swiss! It
>ems that they cannot see a mountain peak without at once
>tting a railway of some kind up it. Often, too, they build a
>tel at the top of it – which is natural enough, I suppose,
>hen one considers the number of visitors who make the
>cent. Unless, indeed, the hotel was there first, which would
>rtainly make the construction of the railway or funicular
>ore understandable. To take people up to the hotel, I mean.
>t, in that case, it is hard to see how the materials and so on
>ere taken up to the hotel in the first place. It is like the chicken
>d the egg, as I said to the hall-porter when discussing the
>oblem with him after breakfast; but he does not, I think,
>nderstand English as well as he would have one believe. He
>mply directed me to the *Speisesaal*, from which of course I
>d only just come. I thanked him gravely, and to spare his
>elings pretended to glance over the letter rack until he went
>way. One says 'thank you' for useless information a good
>any times a day, I find, when abroad. It is all part of the
>me.

We had a splendid day on the Rigi. The journey up the la
to Vitznau is most inspiring, with ever-changing views of t
surrounding mountains and other points of interest, which
did my best to point out to my two charges. But they we
generally on the other side of the boat, as boys so often are.
I chatted pleasantly with Mrs Fitch, who to my surprise turn
out to be on board, and let my conscience go hang. After a
although it is my duty to see that this holiday is educational f
them, in the fullest sense, it is no bad thing to let them broad
their minds on their own once in a way. I am always there,
they need me.

I had not realized, to tell the truth, that Mrs Fitch was
widow, until she told me that she had no one to care for no
I was wondering what to reply when the ship put in at Gersa
to pick up more passengers, and no sooner was this distracti
over than Geoffrey came across to ask a question about m
map, which he had very sensibly borrowed. So the opportuni
was lost. However, as I had not been able to phrase any entire
suitable words of commiseration or consolation, no very gre
harm was done, I dare say. It is only that one likes not to
thought boorish or indifferent.

'The point is,' Geoffrey said, flattening the map on the se
beside me, 'this is supposed to be a lake, isn't it?'

'It is indeed,' I replied. 'With a maximum depth, just abo
where we are now I believe, of over 700 feet. So don't
leaning too far out over the rail, you two, or I shall be aft
you.'

'Then why is it called a "See"?' he demanded, stabbing h
finger on the map. 'Look here, where it says Vierwaldstatterse
See means "sea", surely. It's swanking.'

'My dear boy,' I chuckled, after a quick look round to mal
sure that his remark had not been overheard, 'you really mu
not try to tell these good people what they should call the
lakes. Switzerland has no sea coast, as you know, so wh
should they not use the word "sea" for such waters as the
have? And very fine waters they are, too, are they not?'
concluded, raising my voice.

'They made a good job of it, anyway,' William joined i

abbing at the map as his brother had done. 'Look, it's the
Vierwaldstattersee where we are now, and the Urner See
where it goes round the corner at Brunnen . . .'

'*And* the Kussnachter See in that sort of creek thing,'
Geoffrey said, 'and the Luzerner See or something there, and
the Alpnacher See down here. Golly, it's a swizzle.'

'Five seas in one lake,' William counted. 'It's a good thing
they haven't got a real sea or they'd soon run out of names.'

'And what is your definition of a real sea, young feller-me-
lad?' I asked, to test him.

'Something that's salt anyway, and doesn't keep going
round corners,' he declared, and we all burst out laughing.

'That would include Lot's wife, wouldn't it?' Mrs Fitch
asked innocently.

'Or a bloater,' I added, to keep the fun going.

With one thing and another it was a light-hearted voyage,
and so hot into the bargain that I had to go below before we
reached Vitznau to remove my pullover. We had another good
laugh as soon as we were ashore, when Geoffrey pointed out an
English poster at the railway station saying 'Come to Skeg-
ness!' or some such place, and William wanted to know why
on earth the Swiss should want to go *there*. 'Perhaps they like
to look at a sea that doesn't go round corners,' I said with a
twinkle, though I thought it right to add, when the laughter
had died down, that young people must learn to admire the
beauty of other countries without belittling their own. Mrs
Fitch, for some reason, chose this moment to tell me that I was
an unbelievable pet, a remark which I hope the boys did not
overhear. They sometimes misunderstand grown-up teasing.

At Rigi Kaltbad, about two-thirds of the way to the actual
summit, we left the train for luncheon, on Mrs Fitch's advice,
and fed very comfortably on a terrace off some excellent veal
steaks. We elders drank a bottle of lavaux (a local wine I am
told) – an expense that I think Mr Bennett, my employer,
would have approved, though I shall of course offer to reim-
burse him for Mrs Fitch's share of it. The strong air made me
feel very fit. Looking out over the vista of mountains and down
to the gleaming lake below it seemed a far cry from Dora's

Café in Fenport, where I sometimes have a cup of tea, an
even from Burgrove School, happy though I have been ther
at times. A line or two of poetry, suming it all up, hovered a
the back of my mind, but when I turned to share the though
with the others I found I could think of nothing but an oddly
worded notice about the boys' dirty laundry that was once pu
up on the School Board by a temporary matron. The min
works in curious ways at times.

And so to the summit, the Rigi Kulm itself. 'My goodness !
I could not help exclaiming, when the magnificent view burs
upon us. 'What an amazing sight.' And everybody within ear
shot agreed with me. The boys simply stood and drank it all in
while I quietly spelt out the names of such peaks as I coul
identify from the map and reminded them how with the ai
of trigonometry the height of each one of them could b
accurately determined. Boys are always interested, in my no
inconsiderable experience, to be told how the lessons they ar
learning at school are practically applied in the larger worl
outside, and I was bringing them up gradually from sea-leve
to a series of gradually established trig. points when the inevit
able tiresome bore, whom none of us knew from Adam, inter
vened with the announcement that on a really clear day it wa
possible to see the Flugelhorn, or it may have been the Grunt
stock.

'Indeed !' I said coldly. 'That must be delightful. But we ca
see all the peaks we need as it is, thank you.'

I fear I was a little abrupt, but really ! He took himself of
almost at once, but the spell was broken, and we too made fo
the train, to complete the round trip back to Brunnen, vi
Goldau and Schwyz. 'Well, well, well, well, well !' I said
smiling round at the others, as the train jogged and jolted it
way down between rocky walls. 'We shall all be glad of a cup
of tea when we get in.'

They were silent, however. It seemed odd that they shoul
have nothing to say after what had been, when all is said an
done, a remarkable experience.

A Glimpse of Italy

is no surprise, naturally, to find so many foreigners in
Switzerland, but one had expected them to be Swiss. Or, to
look at it from the Swiss point of view (as I make a point of
trying to do when abroad – when in Switzerland, that is to say,
and of course, *mutatis mutandis*, elsewhere) one had expected
the foreigners to be *English*, which is what we are really, as I
keep reminding the two boys, when we leave our own country.
I mean it is we who are the foreigners, not the other way
round, whereas in fact most of the others here seem to be
Germans and Dutch and Danes and so on. Quite a cosmo-
politan gathering, and very different from the old days when
the English were the great travellers. Still, it all adds to the fun
and has certainly opened the eyes of my two young charges.
'As you see, the English are not the only people in the world,' I
sometimes say to them, to drive the lesson home.
   To give them their due, both Geoffrey and William have
been keen to make the very most of their continental holiday.
'When are we going to spend that Italian money?' they kept on
asking me before we had been here a week, and in the end I
agreed that we would make a little expedition through the St
Gotthard tunnel into Italy. Just for the day, of course. I had
had this plan in mind all along, as a matter of fact, and had the
forethought to bring a few thousand lire with me, a fact of
which the boys happened to be aware. But *having* money does
not necessarily mean that one must *spend* it, as I felt it my duty
to make clear to them. Besides, it does them no harm to be kept
on tenterhooks for a while. Discipline is not always so easy to
maintain while on holiday as at school; one can hardly set
them impositions and so on, in cases of disobedience. But I had

only to say quietly, 'If you do that again I shall not take yo
to Italy, William,' and that was the end of it for half an ho
or more. 'When you've a treat in store for the little devils,' as
wise old colleague once said to me, 'keep it up your sleeve
long as ever you can.'

I decided that Lugano would make a pleasant jaunt, an
we caught the ten-forty-three from Brunnen, arriving at o
destination after a thoroughly Alpine run at twenty-thr
minutes past one. This gave us a good two hours in the pla
before taking the half-past three train which gets back
Brunnen at six-twenty-five, in good time for dinner. The bo
enjoyed the great tunnel, which I confess was a new experien
for me too, and eagerly pointed out to each other the Itali
names on the farther side. The sun seemed to shine with add
warmth as we ran down the southern slopes of the migh
range and I think I dozed off for a while. At any rate the tin
passed quickly, and we were all in high spirits and ready f
lunch as we left Lugano station and strolled to the lakeside
search of a suitable place to eat.

'Look, *ristorante*!' cried Geoffrey. 'How super!'

Then William spotted the word '*impermeable*' in a sho
window full of raincoats, Geoffrey capped it with '*pantalon*
and not to be outdone I silently pointed a finger at the absu
legend '*pizzicàgnolo*' which happened to catch my eye. 'What
it mean?' William demanded, and I was still considering m
reply when Geoffrey suddenly stopped dead in his tracks an
said excitedly, 'I say, Mr Wentworth. They never stamped u
in.'

'Stamped us in?' I retorted. 'Whatever do you mean, boy

'Our passports,' he said. 'You know. Nobody bonked them
and he banged a fist down into his open palm to show what I
meant.

'Nor they did,' William put in. 'Gosh, what a swizzle!'

'Well,' I said, laughing, 'what of it? I dare say as we are onl
here for a couple of hours — '

'How should *they* know?' Geoffrey said. 'Besides, I want
bonked.'

'There's no need to get in a state about it,' I said. 'And please talk sensibly.'

'So do I,' William shouted. 'I want it to say Italy. There's not much point otherwise.'

I was inclined to tell them both not to be silly little fools. If they thought I had brought them all this way simply to have their passports stamped they were no better than babies. But on reflection it did seem a little odd that we had somehow missed the frontier formalities, and of course there was the possibility that when we attempted to re-enter Switzerland there would be a fuss, since we should have nothing to show that we had ever left it or where we had been in the meantime.

'Very well,' I told them. 'If it is as important as all that we must see what we can do,' and I began to retrace my steps, with the idea of inquiring at the railway station. However, we soon spotted a policeman, or *carabiniere* as they say, and to save time I put our little difficulty to him. We had come, I explained, from Switzerland, just for the day, but through some oversight our passports had not been stamped on entry. Would he kindly advise me how to regularize the position?

'*Passaporto?*' he said.

'Yes,' I replied, speaking very slowly and clearly. 'Not stamped. *Sapristi?*'

It was soon clear that he understood little if any English, and having myself no great command of Italian I took my passport from my inside breast pocket and opened it at the page bearing the Swiss entry stamp at Zurich. 'See?' I said.

'*Si,*' he replied.

'Now then,' I went on, squaring my shoulders, 'here' – and I laid a finger on the entry stamp – 'is Switzerland. *Schweiz.* Yes?'

'*Si,*' he said. '*Svizzera.*'

'As you will,' I replied. 'But here,' jabbing my finger on the empty space below, 'no stamp! *Marka? Indorsimento?*'

He nodded his head several times, but I have spent too many years as a schoolmaster not to recognize a look of utter incomprehension when I see one and I therefore brought my clenched fist sharply down on the open passport. 'Bonk!' said, shaking my head to indicate that it had not been done.

'Try bonka,' one of the boys advised. 'They always put a "a" on it.'

The officer smiled vaguely, looking up and down the roa as though for help, and I began again at the beginning 'Schweiz,' I said pointing. 'Svizzera. Yes?'

'Svizzera,' he said. 'Si.'

'Good!' I said. 'Buona! But Italy – Italia – no!'

'Italia,' he agreed, 'no!'

'Well then!' I cried in exasperation. But it was useless. The policeman, with a polite 'Scusa!' took my passport from me flipped over the pages, studied my entry visa for America fo a moment, and handed it back with a bow. 'Come!' he said finally.

We followed him, willy-nilly, for a few hundred yards unti we came to what I surmised, rightly, to be a police station where to my great satisfaction I very soon found myself talkin; to an officer who spoke, on the whole, very good English.

'But Mr Wentworth,' he said, raising his eyes from my pass port, when I had briefly explained the situation, 'Lugano is in Switzerland. There is no need for your passport to be stampee until you cross the frontier.'

'Then we are not in Italy?' I cried, unable to believe my ears. 'God bless my soul! But everybody speaks – the signs – I always thought the St Gotthard...'

'We also speak German in Switzerland, as you know, and we are not, I am happy – we are not, that is to say, in Ger many. We speak French, in the Valais, and we are not ir France. Yes?'

'You also speak excellent English,' I said warmly, 'and you are not –'

'Exactly,' he said. 'Though that is rather different.'

I cannot think, looking back, how I came to make so stupid a mistake. But there it was, and I could only be thankful tha the two boys remained out of earshot during our conversation All the same, I was not out of the wood by a long chalk.

'My two young charges will be sadly disappointed,' I tolc

e official, after apologizing for so unwarrantably wasting his
ne. 'They had set their hearts, for some reason, on having
ly stamped in their passports.'

'So?' he said, smiling. 'It is always the same, when we are
ung. But it is only a few kilometres to the frontier, on the
enaggio road. Would it not be possible – ?'

I glanced at my watch. 'Unfortunately,' I said, 'we have to
tch a train back to Switzerland – to Brunnen, that is to say
at half-past three. And we have not yet lunched. These
rmalities, in my experience, take time.'

'I see,' he said. 'Yes. One moment, monsieur.' He left me to
nfer briefly with one of his colleagues, and returned with an
pression of the greatest delight. 'All is arranged,' he said.
lease to follow me.'

Well, to cut a long story short, the good-natured fellow
ok the three of us out to the frontier post and back. In a
olice car! 'Gosh, we're doing eighty!' young William
outed, and so we were, though it was only in kilometres of
urse. 'You are really extremely kind,' I said to our friend,
it he merely smiled and said, 'Leave everything to me,' which
was only too glad to do. We were stamped out of Switzerland
id into Italy in the twinkling of an eye, and as we stepped
om the farther post on to Italian soil I could not resist the
mptation to raise my hat in the air and cry gaily, 'Well, boys,
hat do you think of that?'

'Whacko!' they both said. 'But it seems funny –'

'Time to be going, if you want any lunch,' I told them, and
a minute and a half, all told, with many friendly grins and
outs of 'Stay a bit longer next time', we were stamped out of
aly again, '*Bonk, bonk, bonk*!' as William aptly put it, des-
ibing our whirlwind progress. 'And one *bonk* to come,' his
rother added, as we approached the Swiss frontier post once
gain.

Here, however, there was an unexpected hitch. Two
istoms men sternly demanded whether we had anything to
eclare – any silks, leather goods, watches, cameras, etc., and
efore I had time to say a word one of them made a dive for

my waistcoat pocket and dragged out my gold half-hunt
'Italian, no?' he said. 'You bought her in Milan just now?'

'That watch belonged to my great-grandfather, young ma:
I replied with some heat, 'and what is more – ' But I sudden
noticed that everyone was laughing, including our policem:
friend, and there was nothing for it but to join in. What
people, eh?

So there it was. The four of us lunched together, at n
expense (or rather at my employer, Mr Bennett's, strict
speaking, though I am sure he would have been the first
authorize the extra expenditure, had he been with us), and
very jolly meal we made of it. 'Any time you are passi:
through Fenport, Hampshire,' I said to our good friend wh
the time came for us to part, 'don't fail to look me up'; and I
promised that he would, or wouldn't, rather. 'I really me:
that,' I added. And so I did.

'The funny thing *is*,' William said sleepily as our tra
climbed up towards Airolo, 'how when we were in Ita
already we had to sort of go out of Switzerland to get into
again. Into Italy, I mean. And then we went out of Italy ar
into Switzerland, so as far as I can see we ought to be :
Switzerland *now*.'

'So we are, William,' I said.

'But in that case – '

'Oh, stow it, Bill!' his brother said, and though I do not :
the ordinary way allow rudeness to pass unchecked, eve
between close relations, I left it at that.

Scotched Rumour

It is good to be back in one's own country again, with solid, sensible words like 'Family Butcher' in the shop windows instead of that absurd *pizzicàgnolo* (which means 'pork butcher', I am told) and policemen in proper helmets. One misses the mountains, of course, and the air, which has been likened, I forget by whom, to champagne. But I feel very fit after the holiday, and the two boys benefited I am sure both mentally and physically. 'They tell me they never had a dull moment in your company,' Mr Bennett very kindly wrote when sending a final cheque which will be more than useful. 'I only wish I could have been with you to share the fun.' Speaking for myself I am thankful that he was not, since I should not have been there had he been able to accompany us. But no doubt he meant it kindly.

Having no further engagements at present I am settling down into the old routine at Fenport, and have no intention yet awhile of renewing my advertisement for temporary employment in *The Times*. One needs a little rest at my age, greatly though I have enjoyed my varied experiences. My three weeks in the heart of Wiltshire, followed by this fortnight abroad, have amply repaid the trifling original outlay, both in money and health. I could eat a horse, as they say.

The second-hand furniture nuisance has died down, I am thankful to say. None too soon, for really it was very difficult to know how to get rid of all the people who brought odds and ends for me to see, and my little cottage is seriously over-crowded. I suppose it was weak of me to buy an egg-collector's cabinet, for I am no oölogist, but at eight and sixpence it was something of a bargain and may well come in handy in the long run. I have a plan for removing the partitions and filing receipts and so on in the drawers. Or I may present it to Burgrove, if the Headmaster approves. We shall see.

Meanwhile the most ridiculous rumours are going about here. My own concerns are no business of anyone else's, and I could see no necessity to tell people here that I was seeking temporary employment, but my absences have been noticed, of course, and the gossips have been busy. 'I hear you were caught trying to smuggle second-hand watches out of Italy,' Mrs Wheeler astonished me by saying, in the full hearing of the tobacconist. 'Was it in aid of this antique business of yours in Wiltshire – or Northumberland, is it?' What a farrago of nonsense! It was all I could do to keep my temper.

'Really, Mrs Wheeler!' I exclaimed. 'I did not think that you, of all people, would listen to such silly talk. If Miss Stephens has been going about – '

'Oh, Mr Wentworth!' I was dismayed to hear Miss Stephens herself exclaim. 'How could you?' She must have followed me into the shop without my noticing, and I had no option but to apologize.

'I am sorry if I appear to have been talking about you behind your back, Miss Stephens,' I said stiffly. 'But upon my soul, the tittle-tattle that goes on in this place is enough – '

'There's so little else to do, you see,' Miss Stephens said. 'We can't all go dashing off to the Continent on mysterious errands. You shouldn't be such a dark horse, Mr Wentworth.'

'Dark horse, indeed!' I began, fingering my tie. 'It is true that I have been in Switzerland for a short spell – '

'Well, I'm glad you don't deny *that*,' Miss Stephens said. 'Or I should have to confound you by producing Myra Fitch's letter.'

'Mrs Fitch!' I cried, colouring despite myself. 'Well, well, well. Good gracious me!'

'She is an old friend of my mother's,' Miss Stephens said, 'and Mother sent on her letter about her holiday. She thought it might interest me, as it said quite a lot about a man from Fenport. It did.'

'Aha!' put in Mrs Wheeler, to my great annoyance. Mrs

itch is a very charming lady, who was good enough to help
e look after the boys on one or two of our expeditions in the
ountains, and naturally we spent my last evening together on
e hotel terrace, admiring the tranquil waters of the lake and
lking over this and that, as one does. Had I been ten years
ounger, I dare say – who knows? – I might have suggested a
roll along the shore, but the night air grows a little chilly after
inner. But it is no business of anybody's that I can see.

'An ounce of Richmond Curly Cut, please, Mr Gooch,' I
id loudly, to show the two ladies that I had no wish to
ontinue the conversation, which seemed to me quite unsuit-
ble for a tobacconist's shop. 'And a box of matches.' But it
kes more than a box of matches, however briskly ordered, to
ersuade Miss Stephens to leave well alone.

'I can give you her address, if you like,' she told me, with an
rchness that I found most distasteful.

'I have it, thank you,' I replied, before I could stop myself,
nd raising my homburg with as much politeness as I could
uster bade them both good morning. The whole affair is
rifling, but it is difficult to get it out of one's mind. One cannot
elp wondering, naturally, what Mrs Fitch said in her letter.
Nothing to my discredit, I'll wager.

So her name is Myra, eh?

To quieten the spate of talk I have thought it best to let it be
nown in the district that I have recently taken one or two
emporary posts, to eke out. One would have preferred to keep
his sort of thing to oneself, but something had to be done to
cotch the rumour (started, I shall always believe, by Megrim)
hat I had become a kind of Queen's Messenger and was likely
o leave for Ankara at any moment. Another theory I heard
being discussed in the Post Office was that I had business
nterests abroad – I wish I had – and that 'this second-hand
urniture racket', as one man had the impertinence to call it,
was only a blind. It was getting beyond a joke. Anyway the
ruth is now out, and the result is that I am being bombarded
with surreptitious gifts of fruit and vegetables and so forth.
People are very kind, but really! I have a sufficiency of means,

as long as I am reasonably careful, and much as I have alway
enjoyed *Cranford* (one of my favourites since I was quite
young man) I do not at all relish the role of a Miss Matty
however well meant the thought behind it. They will be settin
my cottage up as a sweet-shop next! It is hard to know wha
to do, without giving offence, and in any case one canno
return a cauliflower left, without message of any kind, in th
tool-shed. Even when I caught Mrs Wheeler red-handed put
ting a dozen eggs down by the back door she managed to mak
a tremendous favour of it. I mean a favour to her, of course
'I'm simply snowed under with the wretched things, Mr Went
worth,' she told me. 'So if you could *bear* to help me out . . .'
tried to pay for them, although I already had four dozen in th
larder, but she said it was more than her life was worth unde
the Egg Marketing Scheme or some such extravagant rubbish

I don't know, I'm sure. It occurred to me to make repay
ment in kind to some of these good people, and I did manag
to leave a small gate-legged table in the Wheeler's garage an
a pair of brass-bound bellows at Miss Stephens's place, beside
one or two other bits and pieces which relieved the congestio
in my sitting-room. But it was difficult work after dark, an
little good came of the plan in the end. All the pieces wer
recognized and returned, either direct to me or via the peopl
who had sold them to me while the second-hand furnitur
rumour was at its height, and the general belief (which I ha
not the heart to deny) was that the whole thing had been th
work of a practical joker, who had raided my cottage and
distributed my belongings at random. 'And a joke in damn
bad taste, too,' Mr Wheeler remarked to me with a good dea
of heat. One way and another there was quite a fuss, with
everybody doing everything they could to make it up to me. It
is all rather embarrassing, and I often wish I had some sym-
pathetic soul, like Myra Fitch, to talk things over with.

I thought it only civil, in passing, to send her a card – or
brief note, rather; nobody who knows the postmistress here
would send a postcard even on quite ordinary topics, as was
mine I need hardly say – to inquire about her journey home
among other things, and she replied with a very kind letter,

which filled my head with what might have been dangerous thoughts in a less balanced man. What have I to offer a lady after all, even if the thing were feasible, except a small pittance and an outhouse full of vegetables and corner cupboards? Ah well! There it is. I wrote a long reply, not wishing to seem unfriendly, and as luck would have it ran into Miss Stephens on my way to the post. 'Caught you, Mr Wentworth!' she cried gaily, eyeing the envelope in my hand with a great deal of curiosity. 'There are going to be some sad hearts in Fenport when the announcement appears in *The Times*.'

I might have made a sharp reply, had I not caught a glimpse of what looked suspiciously like tomatoes in her bicycle basket. All this kindness, awkward though it is in a way, is quite disarming.

'The only announcement you are likely to see in *The Times*, Miss Stephens,' I said with a smile, 'is that Mr Wentworth is no longer available for temporary employment in positions of trust as he is setting up a greengrocer's shop in Fenport.'

It was rather naughty of me, I suppose, but her confusion was delightful to see. 'Caught *you*, I may say, Miss Stephens!' I added. 'It is very, very kind of you all, but it must really stop. I am quite all right, you know – quite all right.'

'Well,' she said, after a little silence, fiddling with her handlebars, 'we happen to be rather fond of you in these parts, you see. Still, I'll tell them.'

'My dear young lady,' I began, but found it quite impossible to complete whatever it was I had been about to say.

'You aren't going away on any more of these jobs, I hope,' she said. 'Not for a bit, anyway.'

'No, no,' I assured her. 'No. I shall spend the next few months among all my good friends in Fenport.'

I was wrong, however. By the very next morning's post I received to my astonishment a letter from my old Headmaster, the Rev. Gregory Saunders, M.A., telling me that the school was in some difficulty owing to the sudden illness of Mr Thompson and asking whether I would consider tiding them over by returning to Burgrove for the last five weeks of term.

'You shall have your old IIIA mathematical set. Do come!' he wrote.

Well! It did not take me long to make up my mind, as may be imagined. Back to the fray on Monday, eh!

I felt quite boyish as I sat polishing up my mathematical instruments after tea. It will be like old times to feel a piece of chalk between one's fingers again.

Back to Burgrove

grand to be back here again, if only 'to tide us over' as the
admaster puts it. Well, I have tided them over a few diffi-
ties in my time, and I dare say I can do so again. Of course
not the same. One cannot expect to step back into one's
seat at the top of the Common Room tree on the strength
a few weeks' temporary work. Easy does it. 'Tact, Went-
rth old boy!' I said to myself as I shaved this morning.
ct and diplomacy!' And be sure I shall need both. I had
hold myself in pretty tight directly after chapel when I was
nging up my gown in the old familiar cupboard. They've
in a new light-switch, I noticed: one of those pull-down
ngs on the end of a long string, which always seems to me a
– not suggestive exactly. Anyway I don't like them. But it
sn't that. It was a young fair-haired fellow, new since my
e and takes French and History they tell me.
I say,' he said, 'you must be Thompson's stand-in. That's
Rawlinson's peg, if you don't mind my telling you. He's a
touchy, you know.'
Well!
It was on the tip of my tongue to inform this young hopeful
at the peg in question happened to be mine, that I had used
or twenty-seven years (ever since the Lent Term 1933, when
Poole gave up, to be precise), and that if anybody was
spassing it was Rawlinson. But my sense of humour won the
y and I thanked him instead, saying with an assumption of
utmost gravity, 'I am most grateful for the hint. You have
ed me from an irreparable blunder.' I then took my tattered
gown off the peg and hung it up again, with mock humility,

on the farthest peg of all, right in the corner where the rol
up map of Europe before the Great War used to stand.

'That's mine,' the young fellow said.

Still, all the familiar smells are there, and I snuff them
like an old war-horse returning to the fray. The Headmas
in particular, has been most kind and welcoming. 'It is lik
breath of fresh air to have you back with us, A.J.,' he told
to which I replied, jokingly (though to tell the truth I was v
much moved), 'The School hasn't often been short of fresh
surely, Headmaster?' – a reference to the central heat
system, which was always going wrong in my time. But
missed the point, I think. He has grown rather fat in
middle age, and is no longer known to the boys as the Squ
so Rawlinson tells me. Apparently they call him the Ator
Pile, in their modern way, or 'Tommy' for short, though
real name is, of course, the Reverend Gregory Saunders,

I had quite a shock on entering Classroom 4 for my f
period with my old mathematical Set IIIA. The lower part
the wall, a sensible dark green in the old days, has been pain
primrose, of all colours, with a lighter shade above, on so
cock-and-bull theory that boys work better in cheerful s
roundings. Nonsense! Boys work best when they have got th
heads down over their books, with a master in charge w
knows how to keep a firm hand on the young rascals, not wh
they are staring at fancy plastic emulsions. I suppose it is
part and parcel of turning the place into an 'Inspected Scho
which happened as soon as my back was turned. We are
have a second visit from these gentlemen in a week or two, t
Headmaster tells me, and much good may it do us, or them.
is difficult enough in all conscience to teach boys the Theor
of Pythagoras, without being distracted by some Governme
popinjay sitting in judgement on the teaching methods of
man old enough (though by no means inclined) to be his fath

However, what was in some ways an even greater sho
awaited me with IIIA. One's first duty, naturally, is to list t
boys' names. Not that they are not already listed in the ma
book by one's predecessor, but it makes a start and helps o
to get acquainted and so on.

'Call out your names, please, one by one,' I told them, 'beginning from the left of the front row.'

'Do you want them in the form order, sir?' somebody asked.

'Naturally,' I said. 'That is why I said beginning from the left.'

'The top boy sits on the right, sir.'

I was thunderstruck. Boys at Burgrove sit at their desks in the order of the previous week's mark-lists, and in all my experience it has been the rule that the top boy sits on the left, the next boy on his right, and so on down the rows, ending with the bottom boy (who has to wipe the board and do other small chores) at the extreme right of the back row. Any other arrangement leads, in my opinion, to nothing but confusion.

'In my classroom,' I said, 'the top boy sits on the left. Now will you please get yourselves sorted out in the proper order as quickly as possible. And *quietly*! This is a classroom, not an elephant-house.'

It is extraordinary what an amount of noise a dozen boys can make with their feet, but eventually, after I had given a pretty sharp look to a biggish dark boy whom I caught tweaking another boy's ear as he passed, they all settled down again, and I began to write their names in my book as they called them out.

'Henderson,' I repeated, 'Blake, Wrigley . . . With a "W"?' I asked, looking up at the third boy in the row.

'Yes, sir. As in Wrekin.'

To my astonishment it was the boy next to him who answered, that is to say the third boy from the *right* (there being seven desks in all in the front row, as I ought perhaps to have made clear), and I immediately demanded an explanation. 'Has Wrigley lost his tongue?' I asked sharply. 'Or why do you take it upon yourself to speak for him?'

'I *am* Wrigley,' the boy said, looking genuinely bewildered.

'I see,' I said. 'Wrigley, did you not hear me say that you were to sit in your form order *beginning from the left*. Can you not count up to three?'

Wrigley simply stood there, looking helplessly about him, until the boy on the extreme right, who turned out to be

Henderson, kindly put his oar in. 'I think I can explain it, sir,' he said. 'Wrigley thought you meant our left, not yours. We all did, sir. That's why I'm over here where I am now, instead of being where I was when I started, if you see what I mean, sir?'

It is most important that a master should be fair, as well as firm, and believing that there had been a genuine misunderstanding I said no more than 'Very well, Henderson. But understand this, all of you. When I say "left" in this classroom I mean *my* left and nobody else's. Is that clear?'

'What happens if you are speaking with your back to us?' somebody asked.

'Stand up the boy who said that,' I ordered, in the voice I use only when I mean to have no nonsense. A fair-haired boy with glasses, whose face seemed vaguely familiar, rose to his feet a good deal more slowly than he will learn to do when he knows me a little better. 'I only meant – ' he began.

'Your name?' I said sternly.

'Mason, sir.'

'Mason!' I repeated. 'Indeed! Mason, eh? Well, well, well, well. Good gracious me! I see. How old are you, Mason?'

'Eleven and a half, sir.'

There was a fair-haired boy called Mason here in the old pre-war days, with whom I crossed swords on one or two occasions. Not a bad-hearted chap, but a little too inclined to overstep the mark. Indeed at times he was downright insolent, which I am scarcely the man to tolerate. It would be odd, though not of course impossible, if I were now to have the doubtful pleasure of trying to cram the elements of algebra into his son's head.

'May I sit down now, sir?'

Some of the other boys laughed at this, and I very soon spotted the reason.

'You appear to be sitting down already, Mason,' I said. 'So I am afraid I fail to see the point of your question.'

'Oh, so I am sir. I must have done it without noticing. What I mean is, may I have your permission to sit down, sir?'

If I had not been quite certain before, this sort of tomfoolery was enough to convince me of the boy's identity. I was

nxious to have no unpleasantness at my very first period with
IIA, but the sooner this youngster was put in his place the
etter it would be for all of us.

'Mason,' I said slowly, 'I believe your father – All right, boy,
t down now – your father was at this school, I believe, in the
ite 1930's. Is that so?'

'Yes, he was, sir. He told me all about you.'

'Indeed!' I said. 'That must have been very interesting. And
id he tell you, among all the other things, that I was not a
ood man –'

'Oh, no, sir.'

'Not a good man,' I continued, raising my voice, 'to try to
e funny with? Do you happen to remember that, Mason?'

The boy had the impertinence to pretend to be racking his
rains, until I brought him to his senses by rapping sharply on
ny desk with a pair of compasses.

'I expect he did, sir,' he said hurriedly. 'Sir, is it true, sir,
hat you once fell backwards into a kind of basket in the boot-
oom?'

'Be quiet, all of you,' I cried. 'We are wasting far too much
ime. Henderson, where had you got to with Mr Thompson
efore he became ill?' I had forgotten, until the boy I was
ddressing told me his name was Sibling, that the form was
till back to front owing to this misunderstanding about left
nd right, and there was a further tiresome delay while they
ll got themselves back into their original positions.

And even then, as Henderson reminded me, I had still to
ake their names down before we could get started.

'Henderson, Blake, Wrigley with a "W",' I said briskly –
those I have got. Next?'

There was no reply, and I had to repeat the order. But the
ilence continued.

'Come along, come along, wake up!' I said. 'You, there –
vhat is your name?'

'Kingsley,' the fourth boy said, looking frightened, as well
ne might. 'But I'm not really next, sir.'

'Then why are you sitting there, boy?' I thundered, beginning to lose patience. Upon my soul, I began to wish I had my

old IIIA lot back again, muddle-headed as many of them were.

'It's Potter who's next in the order really, sir,' Henderson explained. 'But he isn't here.'

'Why is Potter not here?'

'I don't know, sir. I think he had to go and see Matron.'

'See Matron and die,' somebody sang out. I suspected Mason, but in my profession one has to be on one's guard against prejudice. So I let it go, and went on with my list of names as though I had noticed nothing. Which was just as well, as it turned out; otherwise I might not have got to the last boy before the bell rang for the end of the period.

We must really get down to it tomorrow. Still, the hour was not entirely wasted. As every schoolmaster knows, it is of the first importance to get on terms with one's boys. Let them see what they are up against right from the start, and then – off with a bang!

Getting the Feel of It

Boys always want to know what is the *use* of what one is trying to teach them. Thus they are always more ready to find out how much wallpaper is needed to decorate a room than, let us say, to factorize an expression or follow a theorem involving tangents. I suppose it is natural enough, in a way, and I do my best to point out some of the applications of mathematical laws and principles to modern life. But one has to be on one's guard against being led astray into time-wasting digressions. One tip, that may be helpful to young men just starting out on the long furrow, is to watch your step when the boys begin to lean back and cross their legs. It means that the young rascals are counting on a good ten minutes' break from real work, and is one of the danger-signals that should never be disregarded. I make it a rule to get straight back to x and y as soon as I see it.

This morning's discussion with IIIA about the diameter of the sun (it originated, rather oddly, in a problem we were working on together about the price of eggs) went on perhaps a little longer than I generally permit, but that was because some valuable lessons seemed to me to emerge in the course of it. The importance of angular measurements, for one.

'Was there ever a time, sir,' Wrigley asked, while I was writing some solar dimensions on the board (and finding incidentally that chalk still breaks on the down stroke just as it always did), 'when people thought the sun was no bigger than the earth?'

I could not resist telling them of some of the weird misconceptions of the ancients, and in particular of a remark made by the Greek philosopher Epicurus which has always amused me, namely that 'the sun is about as large as it looks, or perhaps a little smaller'. This made them all laugh, with the exception of young Notting, rather a serious-minded boy for his age.

'Well, isn't it?' he asked.

He seemed genuinely puzzled, so I told the others to be quiet.

'What I mean, sir,' Notting went on, 'if it looked bigger than it does it *would* be bigger, wouldn't it, and if it were smaller than it is it would *look* smaller, so it must be as big as it looks.'

It is not always easy to follow the mental processes of young boys, so I took a turn about the classroom to clear my mind, confiscating a mint humbug from Mason as I passed his desk.

'And how big does it look to you, Notting?' I asked at length.

'Well, I suppose actually,' he replied, holding up a forefinger and thumb, 'about that.'

'Exactly,' I said with a smile. 'About an inch across. And now what about *my* diameter? No, no – that will do, Mason – how big do *I* look? Measure the width of my shoulders in the same way, with your fingers. So!

'You had better do the same, all of you,' I went on, when Notting had satisfied himself that his mathematics master was three times as big as the sun. 'Extend your arms and make a note of my breadth as it appears from where you are sitting. Then we shall soon learn something about the relationship between distance and angular measurement.'

They at once complied, and I was about to warn them to take the measurement with thumb and forefinger, as Notting had done, and not between their first and second fingers, when the Headmaster looked in to ask some questions about cod-liver oil and malt, which I should have thought could have waited till break. He raised his eyebrows on entering, frowned at the boys, and was somewhat curt in his manner when putting his trivial query. There are times when I have scant patience with these headmasterly moods. He should take more exercise, in my opinion.

I was proceeding, after his departure, to demonstrate on the board from figures supplied by the boys how the width of an

ɔbject can be determined by the apparent width of its extremi-
ies at known ocular distances (though I put it more simply, of
:ourse) when I became aware of a faint hum, or buzz, tending
ɔ increase momentarily in volume.

'Who is humming under his breath?' I demanded, swinging
ound on my heel.

Nobody owned up, though the humming continued, and I
:onfess I derived a certain grim enjoyment from the thought
hat this old dodge should be tried out on an experienced hand
ike myself. It is almost impossible to pin down the actual
:ulprit – culprits, rather, since more and more boys join in if
:he thing is allowed to continue. The lips do not move, and the
ıtter immobility of the boys often has an unnerving effect on
young masters. I remember a young Cantab, Griffiths was it?
ɔr Fenner? Some name of the sort – anyway he did not last
long – who reached the point of imagining that the noise was
ınside his own head and actually took pills for it, until Gilbert
:ook him aside in the Common Room. Still, that was all a long
ime ago.

'There will be a serious row,' I told them, 'unless this hum-
ning stops immediately.'

Looking at their bland, expressionless faces (though one or
:wo of the older ones attempted a puzzled wrinkling of the
brows that might have fooled me thirty years ago) I was
ırresistibly reminded of my old IIIA of pre-war days, and very
near burst out laughing despite my annoyance. 'You have had
your last warning,' I said.

'I think it must be an aeroplane, sir,' Mason said.

'No doubt,' I said. 'Could it be the same one your father
heard in similar circumstances, perhaps?'

A boy called Barstow in the back row had the impertinence
to call out, 'It's coming nearer!' and somebody said he thought
it was a Gipsy Major, or some such nonsense, by the sound of
the engine.

'Very well!' I cried, bringing my fist down with a crash on
my desk. 'Since it is impossible to work while this noise continues, we shall all have to make up the time lost after school

hours this afternoon.' And to ram the warning home I osten
tatiously took the time by my watch.

Instantly, as I had expected, the humming ceased.

'He's crashed,' Mason said — a remark that he may ye
regret, when I have made up my mind what to do about it. Fo
the moment my main concern was to waste no more time and
get down to some solid work straight away.

'Open your books at Exercise 37,' I told them brusquely
'and get to work on the first six examples. No, Hopgood, you
may not. Wait till the bell goes, boy. If there are any difficultie
— Well, Blake, what is it?'

'It's the aeroplane, sir.'

For the life of me I could not help following his pointing
finger and there, sure enough, was a plane of some kind. However, it was only a second or two before I recovered my poise.

'I see,' I said. 'How curious that we should hear its noise so
long before it arrived, Blake.'

'It's the speed of it, sir. The waves get left behind or something.'

'I know all about supersonic effects, thank you,' I said
sternly. 'The only difficulty about your ingenious theory is that
the sound arrives afterwards, not before.'

'This must be a subsonic plane, sir,' somebody put in. 'So
it's the other way round.'

'Unless it's flying backwards,' Mason said.

The bell went just then, and saved one or two of them from
what might well have been the surprise of their young lives.
For the time being, at any rate. Later on, we shall see. I mentioned this aeroplane business to Gilbert during break, thinking
it would amuse him to hear how badly this new generation of
boys had mistaken their man. He tells me that the plane flies
over regularly at about 10.30 every weekday morning and his
guess is that the boys take advantage of it, but misjudged the
timing on this occasion. Well, well, well! It begins to look as if
this man Thompson, whose place I am temporarily filling, were
an indifferent disciplinarian, who has allowed the Set to get a
little out of hand. It may be necessary to tighten things up for
a day or two, until they learn where they stand.

Hopgood, it appears, is no relation of the Hopgood II whom I so unfortunately stunned with a *Hall and Knight* back in 1939. This is a relief, really, as I have no wish to have that absurdly exaggerated affair dragged up again, should the boy's parents happen to come down. Not that I have anything to be ashamed of or regret, except that the wrong boy was hit. It is just that the thing is over and done with, as I told Rawlinson pretty straight after luncheon, when the talk happened to turn on the sons of Old Boys. I was a bit put out already, to tell the truth, by an extraordinary remark of the Headmaster's a little earlier. 'I assume,' he said, taking my arm, as we walked down Long Corridor together, 'I *hope*, Wentworth, that it was the Victory salute your boys were giving you this morning. But whatever it was, don't you feel it would be better – '

'We were discussing the diameter of the sun, Headmaster,' I interrupted with some impatience, 'and I really feel that in such matters my judgement is at least as good as that of a classical man. My methods of work, which are founded as you will agree on a great many years' experience – '

'Classical I admit to being,' he said. 'But even a man whose training has been mainly in the groves of Academe may perhaps claim some knowledge of the significance of gestures and the advisability or otherwise of their concerted use by boys during working hours. Or not, Wentworth?'

'Gestures!' I cried, with some heat. 'I know nothing of gestures. I happen to be more interested in the angle subtended by the sun – '

He did not, however, allow me to complete what I had to say.

'God bless my soul, A.J.,' he cried, slapping me with sudden friendliness on the shoulder. 'You have the power to astonish me, even now!'

Having no idea what he was driving at, I took myself off in something of a huff. Still, I think he means to be kind, and it is pleasant, taking one thing with another, to be back in the dear old place.

A Brush with the Inspectors

It has been a tiring week, on the whole. No doubt Her Majesty's Inspectors have their work to do, and for all I know there may be schools that benefit from it, but I could wish that they would do it elsewhere than in my classroom when I am busy. It is a vexatious thing that this visitation should coincide with my brief stint of temporary work here at Burgrove, particularly as the Headmaster has allowed it to throw him completely out of his stride. Fuss, fuss, fuss! Really, for the best part of a week before these gentlemen were due one hardly knew whether one was on one's head or one's heels. Quite apart from all the sweeping and cleaning, which I dare say was overdue, the school piano has been moved five times to my knowledge and is now back in the music room where it started. I should have thought, as I remarked to Gilbert, that if these people want to see the school at work they should see us when we are fresh and at our best, not tired out with re-marking all the boys' hair-brushes in the downstairs washroom. Then, the usual issue of clean blotting-paper, which has always been on a Monday for as long as I can remember, was held back for three days, despite my protests ('They'll hardly give us many marks for industry,' I pointed out, 'if everybody's blotting-paper is as white as driven snow on a *Thursday*,' but nobody would listen to reason), and to cap it all I got wind of a plan to reorganize my own time-table without consulting me.

Of course I went straight to the Headmaster.

'I am told,' I began without preamble, 'that I am not to be permitted to take IIIA in geometry on Thursday morning, but that for some reason I fail to understand they will go to Gilbert

General Knowledge at that time. In all my long experi-
ce – '

'Certain rearrangements have had to be made as you know,
entworth,' the Headmaster said, 'in view of the Inspection
Thursday and Friday – '

'That certain rearrangements *have* been made I know well
ough,' I put in bitterly. 'Whether they have *had* to be made
another matter.'

'You will kindly leave that to my judgement,' he replied, in
one I was inclined to resent. 'I have to consider what is best
the School. It is essential that the Inspectors' report should
a favourable one, particularly with regard to standards of
cipline and methods of teaching.'

'Well?' I said, as he paused. 'I have yet to learn what all this
s to do with the reorganization, without my knowledge, of
normal Thursday time-table, or,' I added (for I am a great
liever in striking while the iron is hot), 'with the appearance
my classroom this morning of a new check duster, which will
t rub out, in place of the old yellow one which will.'

The Headmaster sank into his chair with a weary sigh, con-
ming my growing suspicion that he is no longer really up to
and should begin to think of handing over to a younger man.
had supposed,' he said at length, 'that you would be glad to
spared the worry of having to teach with an Inspector in the
om. However, if you insist on making an – if you prefer to be
spected, so be it. So be it, Wentworth. Only, for goodness'
ke, don't come bothering me about dusters at a time like this,
ere's a good chap.'

I had half a mind to tell him that if he had not bothered
out dusters in the first place I should have had no occasion
mention the matter. But he looked overstrained and in no
ndition to argue sensibly. Besides I had gained my main
int. So with a quiet 'Worry? About an Inspector in my
om? I'll soon settle *his* hash, if I'm not greatly mistaken,' I
nt off to see about the school roller, which had to be moved
hind the cricket pavilion for some inexplicable reason. Upon
y word, there could scarcely be more of a to-do if we were
tting ready for Parents' Day.

As a matter of fact a very unsightly bare patch was left
the grass beside the gymnasium when we had moved the roll
and I was at my wits' end to find something to cover it up un
Gilbert suggested moving the roller back there again. 'It oug
to be just about the right size,' he said with a grin, and thou
I suppose I ought strictly to have referred the point to t
Headmaster it seemed simpler to act on my own initiativ
After all, if the decision was delayed for any length of tir
there would soon be a bare patch behind the pavilion and
should then be between the devil and the deep sea, as t
saying goes. So I called up my helpers again, and as luck wou
have it ran into the Headmaster as we were trundling the thir
back to the gym again. 'Good, good!' he called out. 'That's t
spirit!' Which only goes to show. As far as I can see there is
coherent plan at all. So long as everything is being moved fro
one place to another and back again we are doing all we ca
to prepare for the inspection. It reminds me of the Army, in
way.

'Required to prove,' I announced, throwing a piece of cha
light-heartedly into the air and catching it again before
struck the floor, 'that the exterior angle of a triangle is equ
to the sum of the two interior opposite angles. Yes, Potter?'

I had decided to run over the familiar theorem again, n
for the benefit of Mr Edwards of Her Majesty's Inspectora
who was sitting at the back but because it is only by consta
reiteration that one can implant the basic principles of ge
metry in young minds.

'I don't see how a triangle can have an exterior angle, si
Potter said. 'I thought the whole point of a triangle was th
all its angles were inside.'

In the ordinary way I should probably have told youn
Potter to wait until I had set the whole theorem out on t
board before raising difficulties, but this morning one had
make allowances. I had, as a matter of fact, in a short talk t
day before, warned them all not to be afraid to ask questio
just because a stranger was present, as it would have given a
entirely wrong impression of a lively and not unintelligent S

if they had all sat silent and mumchance throughout. So that Potter was only trying, according to his lights, to carry out my instructions.

'It is true, Potter,' I explained, tossing the chalk up again, 'that a triangle is, by definition, a plane figure bounded by three straight lines – never mind that now, thank you, Henderson; I have another piece – and in that sense may be said to have interior angles only. But if, in the triangle ABC which I am drawing here, I produce BC to any point D, will you not agree that I have made an angle ACD which may fairly be called an exterior angle?'

'I suppose so, yes, sir,' Potter agreed, in that grudging way so typical of boys.

'But it isn't a triangle any longer,' Mason objected. 'It's more of a corner-flag lying on its side.'

I joined in the laughter – which I dare say surprised the Inspector, who is probably more used to the sort of class where boys have to be kept continually on a tight rein for fear of indiscipline. It would do him no harm to see that a friendly relaxed atmosphere is by no means impossible, if the master knows what he is about.

'You remind me of your father, Mason,' I observed jokingly. 'He, if I remember rightly, disapproved of a triangle with squares on each of its three sides, on the grounds that it looked more like three squares joined together with a space in the middle.' I could not resist stealing another glance at Mr Edwards as I said this, to see how he was taking the intimation (not altogether unplanned, I fear) that he was sitting in judgement on a man old enough to be teaching a second generation. But he was looking out of the window with an abstracted air, and it was all I could do not to ask him to be good enough to pay attention.

'In any case, Mason,' I went on, 'if you dislike my producing BC to any point D –'

'To *any* point D, sir?'

'Yes.'

'I see, sir.'

' – to any point D, you will be even more distressed by my next step, which is to draw CE parallel to BA – so.'

One gets a little out of practice, in retirement, at the difficult art of drawing on the board, and I snatched up the duster with the idea of re-drawing CE more nearly parallel to BA, only to find that I had hold of this wretched new check affair, full of dressing, which did nothing more than make an ugly smear in the middle of my diagram.

'Botheration!' I cried, as I think anybody might in the circumstances. 'Where is my old yellow rag?' And I threw the offending article aside on to my desk where, by cruel mischance, it knocked over a vase of daffodils, which had no business to be there in any case. If I had noticed them before I should certainly have had them removed out of harm's way, but one cannot have eyes in the back of one's head when concentrating on teaching.

'Who put those things there?' I demanded, and as nobody answered I put the onus on the top boy. 'Henderson,' I asked firmly, 'do you know anything about this?'

'No, sir,' he said. 'At least – I think there are flowers on all the masters' desks this morning, sir.'

'What in the name of goodness,' I began – but happening to catch Mr Edwards's eye I decided, out of loyalty to the Headmaster, not to complete the sentence. 'I see,' I said. 'Yes, yes. Of course. I was forgetting it was Thursday!' Which was rather a neat way, I flatter myself, of conveying to the Inspector the impression that it was quite the normal thing to have flowers in the classrooms on at least one day in the week.

'Are we going to have them every Thursday in future?' the little blockhead Wrigley asked, and though several of the boys immediately said 'Sh!' the harm was done. I must say, I blame the Headmaster chiefly, for trying to curry favour with these absurd fal-lals, and I only wish he had been present to see two of my boys attempting to mop up the mess with his infernal duster. 'It seems to be waterproof,' one of them rightly said, and in the end I had to send him out for a towel, which turned out to be not much better. 'I'm afraid it's brand new too, sir,' the boy complained. 'I don't know what's come over

place' – upon which I confess I could not for the life of me
exchanging a covert grin with the Inspector. What non-
it all is, to be sure.

his little mishap unavoidably took up a good deal of time
re I was ready to re-draw my parallel line CE, and I could
quite see what Mr Edwards was getting at when he took
side later in the day and expressed his disappointment that
e fifty minutes he was with me I had not managed to
the proof of the theorem I set out to explain.

he proof?' I said. 'There is no great difficulty about that.
e the lines CE, AB are by construction parallel, the angle
is equal to the interior opposite angle BAC, and the
rior angle DCE – I have an envelope somewhere, I
–'

es, yes,' he said. 'I am aware of the proof, Mr Wentworth.
as not myself I was thinking of but the boys.'

h, the boys,' I said, laughing. 'Don't worry your head
it the boys. They know it backwards by this time. Or if
don't they never will.'

see,' he said. 'In that case I find it a little difficult –
aps you wouldn't mind telling me what you feel to be the
c principles of teaching young boys.'

asic principles!' I repeated, raising my eyebrows. 'There
no rules of thumb or short cuts to success in my profession,
Edwards. There is only one essential ingredient that I know
a lifetime's experience.'

ut *that* in your report,' I was tempted to add, 'and smoke
ut I didn't, naturally. Nothing is to be gained by antago-
ng that kind of person.

End of Term

'Well, well, I suppose there can be no harm in it now.'

The boys had been pressing me to tell them something
the old days at the School – the 1930s seem like the begin
of the world to them, of course – and as it was the last lesso
term, when one traditionally relaxes a little, I had half a m
to indulge them. Mason was particularly anxious to know v
the Headmaster used to be nicknamed 'the Squid' – a fact
he learned from his father, I don't doubt – but I was certa
not prepared to go into that. I was never very clear abou
myself, to tell the truth, unless it had something to do with
octopus's habit of concealing itself behind a cloud of
Certainly, Mr Saunders used to put up an unconscion
number of notices on the board in his earlier days, ma
about bootlaces and the wearing of caps on school walks
similar trivia. But then again, I don't know. These things
happen, as often as not.

'I was only wondering,' Mason said, when he saw my fro
'Of course, if it was anything you wouldn't like to – '

'That is not the point, Mason,' I said. 'One does not dis
the Headmaster in the classroom, as you very well know.'

'Like sex and religion,' somebody whispered: an impe
nence that I should have come down on like a ton of bricks
it been a normal working period. I am not easily shocked,
some of these youngsters nowadays seem to me altogether
old for their years.

'The School was a very different place when I first ca
here as a young man,' I went on smoothly, hitching up
gown, 'and by no means so bright and comfortable as it is ne
And I told them, after cautioning two boys for whistling, b

ere was no linoleum in the upstairs passages and only six
asins in the washroom for nearly seventy boys.

'There are only ten now,' Wrigley said.

'And a hundred and eight of us,' Blake added. 'If you count
opgood, that is.'

'You shut up, Admiral,' Hopgood said, momentarily for-
etting my rule that all remarks must be addressed to me. 'I
ash a jolly sight more often than you do.'

'Where the carpentry shed now stands,' I continued, quel-
ng these interruptions with a look, 'there was in the old days
othing but – What is the matter now, Mason?'

The boy was bowed over his desk in a half-crouching posi-
on and appeared to be engaged in some kind of a struggle.

'My tie's caught. In the hinge, sir.'

'Open your desk then and free it, boy,' I ordered. 'Though
ow in the world – '

'I can't, sir. The lid catches me under the chin.'

'Excuse me, sir, but your gown's hitched up.'

'I am aware of that, thank you, Potter,' I said coldly. 'Now,
Mason, I give you exactly ten seconds to get that tie free and
t down properly, or there'll be serious trouble. Ten seconds,
ind!'

'Can I do the count-down, sir?'

I took up a piece of chalk and flipped it into the air. 'We
an easily spend the rest of the period on parallel lines, if you
refer it,' I warned them, taking a significant pace towards the
lackboard.

'Oh, but, sir! Then we shall never meet,' some fool called
ut, and I should certainly have returned to normal teaching
hen and there if the rest of the Set had not promptly told the
ffender to be quiet and begged me to continue with my
eminiscences.

'Please go on, sir. Sir, tell us about the old days.'

'Sir, there was a scimitar in the Museum . . .'

'Tell us about when you threw the hot-water jugs at
Matron.'

'Sir, is it true you shot the Bishop of Saintsbury single-
anded?'

'Oh, stow it, Coutts. I want to hear about the boot-basket

'Sir! Sir! My father said you were looking for your umbrell on a fine night . . .'

'That will do,' I said sharply. 'Quiet everyone, please Wrigley, do I strike you as the kind of man who would thro water-jugs at anyone, Matron or anyone else?'

That silenced them, as I knew it would, and I took advan tage of the pause to unhitch my gown and say a few straigh words to the Set. 'Every school,' I told them quietly, 'has a lo of silly, exaggerated legends about the past, and it appears, am sorry to say, that Burgrove is no exception. I make allow ances for a certain amount of over-excitement on the las morning of work, but I have no intention of permitting m classroom to be turned into a bear-garden. If you cannot si quietly and sensibly – Do you want to leave the room Notting?'

'No, thank you, sir.'

'Then why is your hand up?'

'I wanted to know if I could ask a question, sir.'

'Very well,' I said patiently.

'Thank you, sir.'

The boy said no more. Indeed he casually picked up a penci and began to doodle. So after staring at him for a minute o two in dead silence I rapped smartly on my desk. 'Get on wit it, Notting,' I told him. 'We haven't got all day, you know.'

'Who? Me, sir?' the boy exclaimed, looking up with a innocent air which did not deceive me for an instant. 'I'm sorry, sir. I haven't got a question ready yet, actually. I only wanted to know if I could ask one in case I happened to thin of one later, sir.'

'He wants to sort of bank one, I think, sir,' Mason was kin enough to put in, in his interfering way.

I thought I knew every dodge for wasting time that boys ca get up to, but this was a new one even to me. However, I wa more than equal to the occasion. If he wanted to cross sword with me he would soon find that two could play at that game

'I see,' I said, without raising my voice. 'Very well, Nottin I am delighted to know that you believe in making provisior

he future. Perhaps, that being so, you will have the good-
to write out "I must not try to be funny in class" fifty
s – just in case I happen to want to set you an imposition
, you know.'

he other boys roared with laughter, and I must say it was
could do to keep a straight face myself at Notting's comical
ession of discomfiture. Somebody called out 'Sucks to you,
ty!', and though the expression is one I generally jump on
it go this time. It seemed to me to sum up the situation
er neatly.

eedless to say there was no further trouble, and all the
s listened attentively while I told them the true story of the
the whole School went to the Tidworth Tattoo – or
ild have gone to Tidworth, rather. The bell rang while I
explaining how my own party were somehow misdirected
Aldershot, so the dénouement will have to wait for another
. If there is another time, of course.

Well, Notting,' I said, as I rather sadly collected my books
the last time. 'What do you think now of your question-
king scheme?'

Not much, sir,' he had the honesty to admit, and feeling
he had learnt his lesson I let him off the fifty lines. After
end of term doesn't come every day.

> Burgrove! Burgrove! Through the ages
> Boy and master sing your praise!
> Turn, yea, turn the crowded pages,
> Ne'er forget those happy days!

How true it all is, I reflected as we sang the old song together
End-of-Term Supper, though of course 'through the ages' is
tching it a bit, as Gilbert says, for a school founded in 1907.
l, there is such a thing as poetic licence, is there not? I for
shall not forget 'those happy days', and tomorrow, when I
alone with my own thoughts again in my little cottage at
port, these last few snatched weeks at Burgrove will seem
a dream, I dare say.

All the same, nothing is to be gained by indulging in
talgic self-pity, as though one were an old man with all

one's life behind one, especially as the Headmaster has just
me that it looks very much as if Thompson would be away
several months yet, so that, should I care to consider it . . .
shall certainly turn the matter over in my mind and let
know in a day or two. Temporary assistance, as the He
master pointed out (he does not scruple, bless his heart, to
every possible means of persuasion to get me back), is dev
hard to come by these days. 'I wouldn't dream of asking
if I knew where else to turn,' he said to me; and though
sentiment was clumsily put I knew very well that he was th
ing only of the sacrifice of well-earned leisure that my acc
ance would entail.

In any case I am not likely to be dull during the holid
As a Vice-President of the Football Club there will be this
that to do, no doubt. Then, of course, if I decide to come b
here, I really must brush up my algebra a bit, which
become surprisingly rusty with disuse. I was very near floo
the other day by a problem about the average speed of
cyclists, of all things! And I should not be very surprise
Miss Stephens is after me again about her precious Dram
Society. Life is very far from being over! In fact it seems to
richer and fuller, in many ways, since my so-called 'ret
ment'. What with Switzerland and the Ripleys and one th
and another, not to mention Inspection Week here (thoug
am quite prepared to forget *those* particular 'happy da
School Song or no School Song!), one has been in quite a w

Talking of Miss Stephens, incidentally, I gather from
Fitch (a lady whom I met in Brunnen, as I may have m
tioned), that she (Myra Fitch, that is) hopes to come dow
Fenport shortly with her old friend Mrs Stephens (who is M
Stephens's mother, naturally) to stay with her. To stay v
Miss Stephens, I mean. Anyway, she (Mrs Fitch) tells me
her last letter that she is very excited at the thought of see
me once more.

It seems a strange coincidence that we should meet ag
One can hardly suppose – And yet, I don't know. We shall
There are times when I scarcely know what to think. In cer
eventualities it might even be that my decision whether or

return to Burgrove would ultimately depend on – well, on
rcumstances. At my age one is not a callow youth. Nor is one
doddering old man, with one foot in the grave, if it comes to
1at.

So there it is. Or may be, rather. Back to Burgrove for one
1ore term, or – an engagement of an altogether less temporary
ind? I don't know, I'm sure. Even supposing. But it is nice to
eel that one may yet be of some use, in one way or another.